Cancer Genetics

Cancer Genetics

Donna M. Bozzone, Ph.D.

Consulting Editor,
Donna M. Bozzone, Ph.D.,
Professor of Biology,
Saint Michael's College

CHELSEA HOUSE
PUBLISHERS
An imprint of Infobase Publishing

Chelsea House
An imprint of Infobase Publishing
132 West 31st Street
New York NY 10001

ISBN-10: 0-7910-8818-9
ISBN-13: 978-0-7910-8818-0

Library of Congress Cataloging-in-Publication Data

Bozzone, Donna M.
    Cancer genetics / Donna M. Bozzone.
       p. cm. — (The biology of cancer)
    Includes bibliographical references and index.
    ISBN 0-7910-8818-9 (hc: alk. paper)
    1. Cancer—Genetic aspects—Juvenile literature. I. Title. II. Series.
    RC268.4.B69   2006
    616.99'4042—dc22

CONTENTS

◆

FOREWORD

◆

Approximately 1,500 people die each day of cancer in the United States. Worldwide, more than 8 million new cases are diagnosed each year. In affluent, developed nations such as the United States, around 1 out of 3 people will develop cancer in his or her lifetime. As deaths from infection and malnutrition become less prevalent in developing areas of the world, people live longer and cancer incidence increases to become a leading cause of mortality. Clearly, few people are left untouched by this disease due either to their own illness or that of loved ones. This situation leaves us with many questions: What causes cancer? Can we prevent it? Is there a cure?

Cancer did not originate in the modern world. Evidence of humans afflicted with cancer dates from ancient times. Examinations of bones from skeletons that are more than 3,000 years old reveal structures that appear to be tumors. Records from ancient Egypt, written more than 4,000 years ago, describe breast cancers. Possible cases of bone tumors have been observed in Egyptian mummies that are more than 5,000 years old. It is even possible that our species' ancestors developed cancer. In 1932, Louis Leakey discovered a jawbone, from either *Australopithecus* or *Homo erectus*, that possessed what appeared to be a tumor. Cancer specialists examined the jawbone and suggested that the tumor was due to Burkitt's lymphoma, a type of cancer that affects the immune system.

It is likely that cancer has been a concern for the human lineage for at least a million years.

Human beings have been searching for ways to treat and cure cancer since ancient times, but cancer is becoming an even greater problem today. Because life expectancy increased dramatically in the twentieth century due to public health successes such as improvements in our ability to prevent and fight infectious disease, more people live long enough to develop cancer. Children and young adults can develop cancer, but the chance of developing the disease increases as a person ages. Now that so many people live longer, cancer incidence has increased dramatically in the population. As a consequence, the prevalence of cancer came to the forefront as a public health concern by the middle of the twentieth century. In 1971 President Richard Nixon signed the National Cancer Act and thus declared "war" on cancer. The National Cancer Act brought cancer research to the forefront and provided funding and a mandate to spur research to the National Cancer Institute. During the years since that action, research laboratories have made significant progress toward understanding cancer. Surprisingly, the most dramatic insights came from learning how normal cells function, and by comparing that to what goes wrong in cancer cells.

Many people think of cancer as a single disease, but it actually comprises more than 1,000 different disorders in normal cell and tissue function. Nevertheless, all cancers have one feature in common: All are diseases of uncontrolled cell division. Under normal circumstances, the body regulates the production of new cells very precisely. In cancer cells, particular defects in deoxyribonucleic acid, or DNA, lead to breakdowns in the cell communication and growth control normal in healthy cells. Having escaped these controls, cancer cells can become invasive and spread to other parts of the body. As a consequence, normal tissue and organ functions may be seriously disrupted. Ultimately, cancer can be fatal.

Even though cancer is a serious disease, modern research has provided many reasons to feel hopeful about the future of cancer treatment and prevention. First, scientists have learned a great deal about the specific genes involved in cancer. This information paves the way for improved early detection, such as identifying individuals with a genetic predisposition to cancer and monitoring their health to ensure the earliest possible detection. Second, knowledge of both the specific genes involved in cancer and the proteins made by cancer cells has made it possible to develop very specific and effective treatments for certain cancers. For example, childhood leukemia, once almost certainly fatal, now can be treated successfully in the great majority of cases. Similarly, improved understanding of cancer cell proteins led to the development of new anticancer drugs such as Herceptin, which is used to treat certain types of breast tumors. Third, many cancers are preventable. In fact, it is likely that more than 50 percent of cancers would never occur if people avoided smoking, overexposure to sun, a high-fat diet, and a sedentary lifestyle. People have tremendous power to reduce their chances of developing cancer by making good health and lifestyle decisions. Even if treatments become perfect, prevention is still preferable to avoid the anxiety of a diagnosis and the potential pain of treatment.

The books in the *Biology of Cancer* series reveal information about the causes of the disease; the DNA changes that result in tumor formation; ways to prevent, detect, and treat cancer; and detailed accounts of specific types of cancers that occur in particular tissues or organs. Books in this series describe what happens to cells as they lose growth control and how specific cancers affect the body. The *Biology of Cancer* also provides insights into the studies undertaken, the research experiments done, and the scientists involved in the development of the present state of knowledge of this disease. In this way, readers get to see beyond "the facts" and understand more about the process of biomedical research. Finally, the books in the *Biology of Cancer* series provide information to help readers make healthy choices that can reduce the risk of cancer.

Cancer research is at a very exciting crossroads, affording scientists the challenge of scientific problem solving as well as the opportunity to engage in work that is likely to directly benefit people's health and well-being. I hope that the books in this series will help readers learn about cancer. Even more, I hope that these books will capture your interest and awaken your curiosity about cancer so that you ask questions for which scientists presently have no answers. Perhaps some of your questions will inspire you to follow your own path of discovery. If so, I look forward to your joining the community of scientists; after all, there is still a lot of work to be done.

Donna M. Bozzone, Ph.D.
Professor of Biology
Saint Michael's College
Colchester, Vermont

1

MOON CHILDREN

KEY POINTS

♦ Cancer is a disease in which the normal social behaviors and interactions of cells do not work properly.

♦ Cancer cells and normal cells differ in how they communicate, stick to other cells, and proliferate, or grow.

♦ A relatively small number of categories of molecules regulate normal cell behavior. In cancer cells, one or more of these molecules malfunction. These molecules are all produced because of the actions of genes. Therefore, cancer is the result of gene malfunctions.

XERODERMA PIGMENTOSUM AND ULTRAVIOLET LIGHT

According to her mother, Logan had always had very beautiful skin. Since Logan's family lived in Florida, her parents were careful to avoid exposing their daughter to excessive sunlight; they wanted to protect

1

her lovely skin. Nevertheless, by the time Logan was 10 months old, her parents noticed that her skin always looked tan and was quite dry. Despite continuing to follow ordinary precautions to limit sun exposure, four worrisome spots appeared on Logan's head. These spots grew in size and changed color—two symptoms that alarmed her parents. At first, Logan's pediatrician said nothing was wrong, but he advised Logan's parents to watch the spots for any additional changes. The spots did not improve and, to Logan's parents' dismay, she was diagnosed, at the age of two, with **xeroderma pigmentosum (XP).** XP is a rare disease in which exposure to **ultraviolet (UV) light** can lead to skin **cancer**, which can eventually lead to death. Logan and other children or adults with XP must live largely indoors, taking great care to avoid all exposure to UV light. Only by living as "Children of the Moon" can individuals with XP minimize their risk of developing potentially fatal skin cancer.

XERODERMA PIGMENTOSUM IS CAUSED BY AN INHERITED GENETIC DEFECT

Jeff Markway, a 13-year-old boy from a family of seven children, noticed a golf ball-sized lump on his arm. He showed it to his mother. Concerned, she rushed Jeff to the doctor. At first, everyone thought the lump was just a **cyst**. When the physician opened the lump to drain the fluid, he was shocked to see a solid mass of cells instead of liquid. He realized that it was not a cyst at all, but a **malignant melanoma**, the most severe type of skin cancer. Jeff was placed under the care of Henry Lynch, a physician and cancer researcher. After careful examination, the cause of Jeff's **tumor** was identified: He had XP. Dr. Lynch examined the rest of Jeff's family and four of Jeff's siblings were also diagnosed with the rare illness. In all, five out of seven children in Jeff's family were diagnosed with a rare disorder that occurs in only one out of every 250,000 people. Dr. Lynch believed the reason there were so many XP children in the same family was clear—XP is a disease that can be inherited. Something was wrong with Jeff's parents' **DNA** (deoxyribonucleic acid). Although they don't have XP themselves, their children inherited this **mutation**, or alteration, in the normal DNA sequence from each of their parents and so developed XP. Dr. Lynch wrote a paper about the unusual incidence of XP within the Markway family.

In the early 1960s, research had been done with bacteria to see whether UV light had any effect on the bacteria's DNA. The results of these experiments not only demonstrated that UV light did damage to the bacteria's DNA but also demonstrated that the bacteria were able to repair the DNA damage. University of California cancer researcher James Cleaver wondered whether human cells would respond to UV light in the same way bacteria did. Cleaver had read Lynch's paper describing the Markway family and speculated that the problem with the Markways' cells (and those of other XP patients) was that those cells were not able to repair damaged DNA.

Cleaver tested this idea experimentally. First, he demonstrated that UV light damaged the DNA of both normal and XP cells. Then he showed that normal cells could repair the UV-induced damage, but XP cells were unable to do so. Because XP patients are not able to repair UV-induced DNA damage, mutations can't be fixed. In fact, they accumulate. Because some of these mutations are in **genes** that influence or regulate the normal behavior of cells, including cell division, there is a dramatic increase in the risk of cancer in any cells that are exposed to UV light. Skin is most vulnerable because it is the tissue most often exposed to UV light. XP individuals under the age of 20 have a 1,000-fold increase

Figure 1.1   A child with xeroderma pigmentosum must wear a protective suit specially designed by NASA to avoid dangerous exposure to ultraviolet radiation from the sun. *(AP)*

in the incidence of skin cancer compared to people who don't have XP. Also, the **median** age of XP patients' first incidence of skin cancer is eight years old, while in non-XP individuals it is 58 years old. The dramatic increase in the risk of skin cancer in XP patients clearly shows the importance of DNA repair in the prevention of cancer. This finding suggests that normal gene function is essential for cancer prevention and that altered genes play a role in the development of cancer. What part do genes exactly play in the prevention or development of cancer?

To answer this question, we need to examine how normal and cancer cells behave both in the body and in **cell culture,** or **tissue culture**.

BEHAVIORS OF NORMAL CELLS AND CANCER CELLS

In order to function in a normal and healthy manner, the body has many mechanisms to control the behavior of its cells. In particular, very careful regulation is maintained of the production of cells; their **differentiation,** or specialization, into specific types of cells, such as brain, lung, or muscle cells; and whether cells live or die. Any failure to balance the number of cell births and cell deaths can lead to abnormal **proliferation** or production of any type of cell in the body, which can result in cancer. Because the body is made up of many different types of specialized cells, any one of which can start developing into cancer, there are hundreds of different types of cancer. Although the many varieties of cancer may make it seem difficult to understand, prevent, diagnose, and treat this disease, most or even all cancers have some features in common. The primary characteristic of all cancers appears to be a change in the functioning of at least one gene that is essential for regulating the social interactions of cells in tissue, an organ, or the body.

Culturing, or the process of growing both normal cells or cancer cells outside of the human body, has advanced our understanding of how normal and abnormal cells function. The mechanisms that regulate cell division, cell communication, how cells stick together to form tissues, cell differentiation, cell migration, and cell survival are defective in cancer cells. Normal cells exhibit a **density-dependent inhibition** of cell proliferation—when the population of cells reaches a certain number, cell division stops. Similarly, normal cells demonstrate

SPOTLIGHT ON CANCER SCIENTISTS
ALEXIS CARREL (1873–1944)

Although it is easy to observe cancerous tumors in tissues and organs of the body, a different approach is needed to study individual cancer cells so that we can learn how they function and behave. One very powerful tool developed to answer questions about cancer cells is the cell or tissue culture, which allows scientists to observe the growth of cells or tissues under controlled circumstances in a laboratory. French scientist Alexis Carrel was one of the first people to **culture** cells from warm-blooded vertebrates and from a type of tumor known as a **sarcoma**.

Figure 1.2 Alexis Carrel pioneered culturing cells outside the human body. *(NIH/NLM)*

Born in Lyons, France, in 1873, Carrel was the eldest of three children. His father, a textile manufacturer, died when Carrel was five years old. Carrel was then raised by his mother, who was a lacemaker. Carrel attended the University of Lyons, where he earned two bachelor's degrees (1889, 1890) and a medical degree (1900). He stayed

contact-inhibition, a behavior in which cells will divide until they create a smooth single layer of cells, but will stop dividing when they physically touch a neighboring cell. Cancer cells display neither density-dependent

in Lyons to perform experimental research in surgery. Some people say that it was the assassination of the president of France in 1894 that gave Carrel's research its focus. The president had been mortally wounded and bled to death because no one knew how to repair a torn artery. Carrel was determined to develop a way to prevent anyone from dying in this manner again. He practiced sewing with tiny needles and very fine silk thread, like those he had seen his mother use in her lacemaking. At first he sewed on paper. Later, he worked on animals. In 1902, he published a paper describing the successful end-to-end attachment of blood vessels.

Carrel moved to the United States in 1904 and continued his successful research. In 1908, he devised methods for transplanting organs. In 1910, he reported that blood vessels could be kept in cold storage for long periods and then used for transplantation. During World War I (1914–1918) Carrel and a biochemist named Henry D. Dakin developed a method to treat and prevent infection of war wounds. Carrel made enormous scientific contributions to the fields of cancer research, transplantation, surgery in general, and heart surgery in particular. He received many awards, including the 1912 Nobel Prize in Physiology or Medicine. His political and social views, however, made him a controversial figure. Carrel publicly supported **eugenics**, the selection of "superior" people for breeding; advocated anti-Semitic ideas; and admired German Nazi dictator Adolf Hitler. During World War II (1939–1945), Carrel was accused of collaborating with the Nazis. However, he was never tried on these charges because he died of a heart attack in November 1944.

inhibition of cell proliferation nor contact inhibition. As a consequence, cancer cells continue to proliferate, move over neighbors, and create disordered patterns of growth.

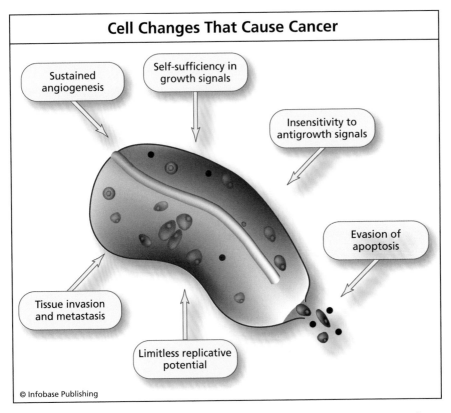

Cell Changes That Cause Cancer

Sustained angiogenesis

Self-sufficiency in growth signals

Insensitivity to antigrowth signals

Evasion of apoptosis

Tissue invasion and metastasis

Limitless replicative potential

© Infobase Publishing

Figure 1.3 Changes to normal cell function lead to cancer. When proper cell operations cease, abnormal cell growth causes a tumor to develop.

Specific biological molecules called **growth factors** must be added to cultures for normal cells to proliferate. Growth factors are small molecules, usually proteins, that act as chemical signals to trigger cell division. It is likely that many cancer cells either do not have as great a need for added growth factors as normal cells do or they can make their own growth factors and stimulate their own cell division. This might be why cancer cells continue to divide. Another possibility is that cancer cells don't need extracellular growth factors at all because some part of the response pathway triggered by the growth factor is abnormal and "stuck on," so that cell division continues unchecked.

If cells simply divided in an uncontrolled manner but stayed at the site of origin, the resulting **benign** tumor would be a lot less dangerous than a malignant, **invasive** tumor that can **metastasize**, or spread, to other locations in the body. Several cell behaviors influence whether a tumor will metastasize successfully. First, cancer cells are less adhesive than normal cells. The surface molecules in cancer cells that attach cells to one another are reduced in number or do not function properly. As a result, cancer cells can detach and leave the tissue in which they originated. Since cancer cells do not exhibit contact inhibition, they readily crawl over other cells. Normal cells, on the other hand, remain attached to their neighbors and, as mentioned above, they exhibit contact inhibition and stop migration once they contact another cell.

Second, cancer cells secrete chemicals called **proteases** that digest the proteins that help hold cells and tissues together. A cancer cell that has detached from its neighbor can use its proteases to "burn" a hole in a tissue and spread into new areas of the body. Cancer cells that manage to enter the circulatory system can travel through the bloodstream to other locations in the body and produce **secondary tumors**. The cell's journey from the original tumor to colonize other tissue is quite arduous; only 1 in 10,000 cells that makes the attempt survives.

Third, the cancer cells that do manage to establish secondary tumors will not be able to produce a cell population beyond a certain size (approximately one million cells or a tumor 0.08 inches [2 millimeters] in diameter) unless the tumor establishes a blood supply. Cancer cells are able to secrete **angiogenic growth factors** that promote the formation of new blood vessels, thus connecting the tumor to the body's blood supply and allowing it to obtain nutrients and oxygen.

Another characteristic that most normal cells do not share with cancer cells is that normal cells stop cell division and differentiate, or specialize, to create specific cell types. In contrast, many cancer cells fail to differentiate and remain instead in an abnormal "embryo-like" state in which they continue to divide.

Finally, normal cells have a finite lifespan: They are born, live, and die. Several types of cells in the body are continually lost by **apoptosis**, or programmed cell death, and are replaced by new cell division and differentiation. Examples include the cells that line the inner surface of the small intestine, certain types of immune system cells, and the skin. In culture, normal cells are only able to undergo

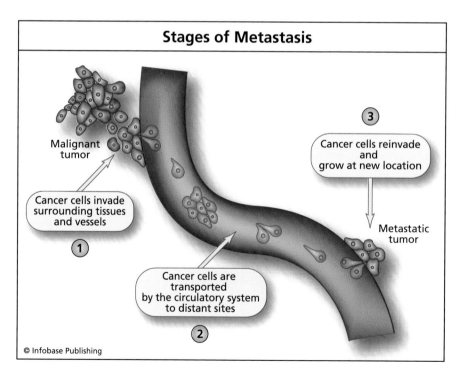

© Infobase Publishing

Figure 1.4   Metastasis is the process by which cancerous cells spread to other parts of the body.

a certain number of cell divisions, usually around 50, before they die. Cancer cells, on the other hand, are essentially **immortal**. In fact, cancer cells that were isolated in 1953 from a cervical tumor continue to survive in culture after more than 50 years. Cancer cells do not die because they fail to heed the cellular signals that control apoptosis. DNA damage triggers programmed cell death in normal cells so they can avoid the negative effects of mutations and faulty genetic instructions. When cancer cells ignore commands to self-destruct, they accumulate mistakes in their DNA, leading to dire consequences, such as metastatic tumors.

GENES INFLUENCE THE BEHAVIOR OF BOTH NORMAL AND CANCER CELLS

The careful orchestration of the cellular societies that comprise our organs, organ systems, and bodies relies upon mechanisms that regulate cell proliferation, communication, and differentiation. Although the list of all the cell behaviors that influence whether a cell is normal or cancerous appears to be quite complex, in fact, these seemingly disparate characteristics are controlled by seven categories of molecules.

First, there are **signal molecules** that tell cells to divide. The signal molecule exerts its effect on the cell by triggering the first of many steps in a communication **pathway** inside the cell. (A pathway is simply a series of interconnected steps or events.) Specifically, the signal molecule binds to the second component of this pathway, a **receptor molecule** that is either on the cell surface or in the cytoplasm. This receptor is the second category of molecules that control cell behavior.

The third category is a molecule called a **signal transducer**. This molecule takes the information the cell acquires when the signal

SPOTLIGHT ON CANCER SCIENTISTS
LEONARD HAYFLICK (1928-   )

In the late 1800s, scientists thought that organisms died of old age because tissues and organs wore out. They figured that parts of the body aged because the ability of cells to undergo division to replace old tissues was "not everlasting but finite."[1] Nobel laureate Alexis Carrel directly challenged this idea when he said that cells in culture were immortal. Dr. Leonard Hayflick resolved the question of whether cells have a finite lifespan in culture.

Born in 1928 in Philadelphia, Pennsylvania, Hayflick earned his Ph.D. in 1956 from the University of Pennsylvania. After completing his degree, Hayflick went to the University of Texas at Galveston to work in the lab of Charles M. Pomerat, one of the world's leading specialists in tissue culture. Hayflick then returned to Philadelphia to run the cell culture laboratory at the Wistar Institute and to study human cancer. During this time, Hayflick discovered that normal cells have a finite lifespan—they would only divide a certain number of times and no more.

During one of his first experiments, Hayflick grew human embryonic cells in culture and exposed them to extracts from cancer cells to see if he could cause cancer in the normal cells. To his surprise, the cells stopped growing. At first, Hayflick thought he had made a mistake. After all, this result contradicted what was previously known about the ability of normal cells to divide "forever" in culture. Over the next three years, Hayflick did many more experiments. One experiment that supported Hayflick's idea that cultured cells have a limited lifespan involved mixing male cells that had divided 40 times in culture with female cells that had divided 10 times. Chromosomes are the cellular structures that contain the physical information for inheritance; because the **chromosomes** of male and female cells can be easily identified, it was possible to tell the two types of cells apart The results of this experiment were very clear. The "older" male cells in the culture stopped dividing long before the "younger" female cells did. Hayflick went on to show that one of the major differences between normal cells and cancer cells was that, when cultured, normal cells have a finite lifespan whereas cancer cells do not. Cancer cells are immortal.

Hayflick's findings were so different from what scientists believed to be scientific fact, that the paper he wrote describing his research was rejected by the *Journal of Experimental Medicine*. Fortunately, the editors of the journal *Experimental Cell Research* chose to publish it. Hayflick's work, which established the field of cellular **gerontology**—the study of aging at the cellular level—was just the beginning of the doctor's long and productive research career. Hayflick has continued trying to figure out how normal cells can determine their ages and how this process goes wrong in cancer cells. He also developed a human cell **strain** (WI-38) that is used in research labs throughout the world. This strain has also been used to make most human virus **vaccines**, including one for **rubella.** Hayflick also succeeded in producing the first oral **polio** vaccine that could be made by cells in culture and successfully established methods to culture **mycoplasma**, the organism responsible for walking pneumonia.

Leonard Hayflick has been awarded more than 25 major honors and prizes for his work. He is currently professor of anatomy at the University of California, San Francisco, School of Medicine.

molecule binds to the receptor and produces another molecule inside the cell that continues to pass along the information.

The fourth category consists of molecules called **transcription factors**. These regulate which genes are being used in the cell and, consequently, what the cells will look like and how they will behave.

The fifth category contains **apoptotic proteins** that tell damaged cells to commit suicide, or are programmed to die.

The sixth category has molecules that directly regulate the mechanisms of cell division.

Finally, the seventh category of molecules are the proteins that repair DNA damage.

In normal cells, all seven of these groups of molecules function properly. In cancer cells, however, one or more of the categories do not. Since the information for making all of the regulatory molecules in all seven groups is in the DNA sequences of specific genes, this means that in normal cells, these genes all work properly, but in cancer cells they do not. In other words, normal cells have the genes code for normal proteins, whereas in cancer cells, altered versions of these normal genes code for abnormal proteins. **Coding** (also called encoding) is the process by which genetic information is assigned to a protein to determine that protein's function. Thus, at the heart of the cellular mechanism of cancer are categories of improperly functioning genes.

The chapters that follow will consider the genetics of cancer in the broad sense, starting with a look at how cancer genes were discovered and then exploring the specific types of genes and genetic defects that cause cancer including **oncogenes**, faulty **tumor suppressor** genes, chromosome abnormalities, and inherited cancer genes. They will examine the idea that multiple genetic changes, rather than a single change, are required for **carcinogenesis**, and then review what the research about cancer genetics can tell us about the detection, prognosis, treatment, and prevention of cancer. Finally, future questions and challenges in this critically important area of biomedical research will be discussed.

SUMMARY

In order to function in a healthy manner, the body must carefully regulate the behavior of cells. Specifically, it is essential that cell proliferation, cell communication, cell adhesiveness, cell differentiation, and cell death are all monitored, balanced, and controlled. Cancer is a disease of uncontrolled cell division. It results when cells no longer follow the constraints imposed on them by other cells. Only seven types of molecules ensure normal cell behavior. If one or more of these molecules fail to work correctly, cancer can develop. Because each of these molecules is encoded by genes, cancer is ultimately a disease of abnormal gene function.

2

How Were Cancer Genes Discovered?

KEY POINTS

- The study of viruses that cause cancer revealed the existence of oncogenes.

- Oncogenes are cancer-causing genes.

- Cells contain proto-oncogenes that can be changed into oncogenes.

- There are more than 100 different types of proto-oncogenes. Each contains codes for a protein that plays a role in regulating normal cell behavior.

- Cells contain tumor suppressor genes that inhibit cell division.

- Mutations in tumor suppressor genes often result in cancer.

- The inability to repair DNA or chromosome damage can lead to cancer.

DISCOVERY OF ONCOGENES

In 1911, American pathologist Peyton Rous made an amazing discovery when he demonstrated that a type of cancer found in chickens was caused by a **virus**. Although the significance of his work was largely unappreciated for most of Rous's life (he was finally awarded the Nobel Prize for Physiology or Medicine in 1966 when he was 86 years old), this observation was actually the first step of many that revealed the existence of cancer genes. In fact, it was thanks to the discovery of the **Rous sarcoma virus** (**RSV**) and other cancer-causing viruses that scientists obtained the tools they needed to tackle the question of the genetic control of cancer.

Dr. Peter Vogt and Dr. Steven Martin decided to study RSV directly to see if its ability to **transform** cells, or make them cancerous, was somehow built into the RSV's genes. By the time their research was done in 1970, scientists had learned that genes are made up of the molecule DNA and that DNA has the information needed to direct the synthesis of **proteins**. (Proteins are essential components of cell structure and function.)

Vogt and Martin isolated mutant forms of RSV that were capable of infecting, but not transforming, cells under certain culture conditions. One of the mutants was temperature sensitive. At 95°F (35°C) the virus was capable of transforming cells, whereas at 107.6°F (42°C) it wasn't. If cancerous growth was initiated at 95°F (35°C) and then cultures were subsequently incubated at 107.6°F (42°C), the cancerous growth stopped. Evidently, the virus makes *something* that is responsible for the start and maintenance of cancerous growth. Unlike normal RSV, the temperature-sensitive mutant made a protein that was itself sensitive to temperature. At higher temperatures, the protein failed to function and the cancerous state could not be maintained in infected cells.

Another type of mutant RSV was unable to transform cells at any temperature. This mutant had a **deletion**, which means that it was missing a piece of genetic material. Analysis of RSV revealed that the virus has only four genes. Three of these genes are necessary for the virus to reproduce itself and one, called *src*, is responsible for cell transformation. In the temperature-sensitive mutants, the *src* gene is altered in such a way that it codes for an abnormal protein. In the deletion mutant, a functional *src* gene is actually missing from the virus. Considered together, these studies demonstrate that *src* is a gene that causes cancer.

The results of any good experiment not only answer questions but suggest new ones as well. In this case, a logical idea to pursue was whether cancer genes are found only in tumor viruses or whether our cells have genes like *src* that can switch them from normal to cancerous growth. It is noteworthy that the viral gene managed to take over the control of a normal cell function, namely cell division. Is it possible that at the root of human cancers are normal cellular genes that have simply gone wrong?

Dr. Harold Varmus and Dr. J. Michael Bishop, then both working at the University of California, San Francisco, decided to pursue these questions by studying the *src* gene itself. They reasoned that *src* might be found in the DNA of normal cells. After all, Vogt and Martin's experiments had showed that *src* was not something that the virus needed to complete its own life cycle. Varmus and Bishop examined the DNA of normal chicken cells as well as the DNA of other types of birds. In all cases, they were able to show that the *src* gene is a normal part of the DNA. Varmus and Bishop also looked at the cells of other types of vertebrates, including humans, and found that the *src* gene was present in all of them. Apparently, *src* is a normal cellular gene that at some point in the distant past was accidentally packaged into a virus during its life cycle thus creating the **oncogenic**, or cancer-causing, RSV. The inclusion of oncogenic genes in previously normal viruses was an evolutionary accident.

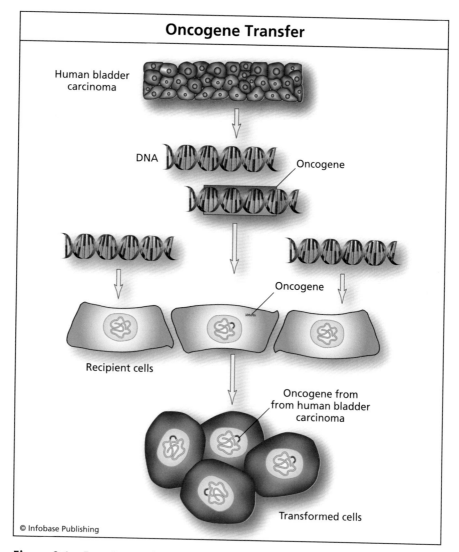

Oncogene Transfer

Human bladder carcinoma

DNA

Oncogene

Oncogene

Recipient cells

Oncogene from from human bladder carcinoma

Transformed cells

© Infobase Publishing

Figure 2.1   Experiments have proven that human cancer cells, which contain an oncogene, transfer a cancer-causing gene when placed in contact with the normal cells.

Once it had been demonstrated that RSV carries the *src* gene that is found in all normal cells, scientists wondered whether other tumor viruses also contained cancer genes and, if so, whether these cancer genes were found in normal cells, too. In 1979, Dr. Diana Sheiness, then at the University of California, San Francisco, showed that another type of chicken tumor virus, called MC29, contains the cancer gene *myc*. Additional experiments verified that the *myc* gene was found in normal cells, just as *src* was.

Direct evidence that cancer can be caused by improperly functioning cellular genes, and not just by stray cellular genes introduced by viral infection, came from experiments done in 1979 at the Massachusetts Institute of Technology (MIT) by Dr. Chaiho Shih and Dr. Robert Weinberg. These scientists took normal cells, treated them with a **carcinogen** (a substance that causes cancer), and produced cancer cells as a result. Next, they removed DNA from the cancer cells they had produced and inserted it into a second set of normal cells. Some of these recipient cells were transformed into cancer cells by the added cancer DNA. In a related experiment done at MIT in 1981, Weinberg and Dr. Geoffrey Cooper showed that the DNA isolated from a human bladder cancer could also transform cells in culture. All of these findings showed that transferring an active cancer gene could cause cancer in the recipients even if no virus was ever involved. Shih and Weinberg isolated the gene from their study and identified it as the **oncogene** *ras*.

Src, *myc*, and *ras* were the first of many examples of normal vertebrate genes that could be hijacked by viruses and, when reintroduced into another cell, could cause cancer. There are actually more than 100 different types of normal cellular genes, or **proto-oncogenes**, that can become oncogenes. Proto-oncogenes encode for proteins needed for the regulation of normal cell behaviors, including communication, division, survival, and differentiation. The disruption of normal proto-oncogene function is implicated in the development of all cancers.

DISCOVERY OF TUMOR SUPPRESSOR GENES

In the eighteen hundreds, German scientist Theodor Boveri predicted that an "excess of chromosome function" could lead to cancer. In other words, Boveri thought that the inherited instructions packaged in the chromosomes directed the production of some substance or substances that could cause cancer. The discovery of oncogenes supports Boveri's hypothesis. The proteins encoded by the oncogenes do indeed cause cancer by actively enhancing cell proliferation in some way. (Oncogenes are something like a car accelerator that is stuck in the "on" position.) Boveri also predicted that "deficiencies in chromosome function" could lead to cancer. This hypothesis suggested that some genes encode for proteins that inhibit cell proliferation. When something goes wrong with these tumor suppressor genes, which are like the brakes of a car, cell division can occur in an unregulated manner.

Was Boveri correct? Are there tumor suppressor genes that normally act as brakes on cell division and do these brakes sometimes fail, leading to the development of cancer?

An experiment that addressed Boveri's idea of deficiencies was done by Dr. Henry Harris in 1969. Harris fused normal cells with tumor cells, creating cells that had the chromosomes of both types of cell. Amazingly, the hybrid cells were not cancerous. Evidently, the normal cells were producing something that inhibited cancer. What it was remained to be discovered. These hypothetical cancer-inhibiting genes were

SPOTLIGHT ON CANCER SCIENTISTS
ROBERT A. WEINBERG (1942-)

Born in Pittsburgh, Pennsylvania, in 1942, Robert Weinberg is an internationally recognized authority on cancer and the genes that regulate this disease. After graduating from high school in 1960, Weinberg began his long relationship with the Massachusetts Institute of Technology (MIT). He earned his bachelor's degree at MIT in 1964 and his Ph.D. in 1969. After earning his doctorate, Weinberg did research at the Weizmann Institute in Israel and at the Salk Institute in California. He returned to MIT in 1972 and has never left. He is now a professor of biology as well as a founding member of the Whitehead Institute for Biomedical Research.

Right around the time that Weinberg completed his Ph.D., President Richard Nixon "declared war" on cancer. At first, a lot of research effort focused on the search for viruses that were then believed to cause human cancer. Although some cancers are, in fact, caused by viruses, most are not. Still, this research yielded important results regarding genes and cancer. In 1975 and 1976, scientists J. Michael Bishop and Harold Varmus

called tumor suppressors. Eventually, molecular analysis identified several specific suppressors. These tumor suppressors encode for proteins that normally inhibit cell proliferation or survival. In many cases, the tumor suppressor genes inhibit the same pathways that are activated by oncogenes. A failure of tumor suppressor genes ordinarily results in the development of cancer. In fact, the inactivation of tumor suppressors is seen in most, if not all, cancers.

discovered oncogenes—genes that cause cancer—in animal cells. In 1981, Weinberg and Cooper made the critical discovery that human cancer cells also harbored oncogenes. Specifically, they were the first to isolate *ras* oncogenes and characterize the specific mutation. Weinberg and his coworkers were also the first researchers to isolate a specific human tumor suppressor gene, called *RB*.

Figure 2.2   Robert Weinberg was among the first scientists to undertake extensive research of oncogenes. (*AP*)

Today, Weinberg continues his research into determining how oncogenes, proto-oncogenes, and tumor suppressor genes fit together in complex regulatory pathways that control cell proliferation. His research program also focuses on the mechanisms responsible for cell aging and on determining how cancer cells acquire the ability to invade other tissues.

CANCER IS A GENETIC DISEASE

The instructions for inheritance or genes are composed of DNA. The information in the DNA is the consequence of its molecular structure. DNA is made up of several types of chemical subunits: the sugar deoxyribose and phosphate, which hook together to make a ribbon-like structure, and four types of nitrogen-containing bases that are abbreviated A, T, G, and C, which attach to the sugar phosphate ribbon and stick out like little plates. The information in the DNA actually derives from the sequence and order of these four bases. The order of these bases provides information in a manner analogous to the way the letters in a word provide different meanings depending upon their order; for example, *rats* versus *star.* Specific combinations, or sequences, of these bases, A, T, G, and C, tell the cell what kind of protein to make.

Cancer can be thought of as a genetic disease in the sense that DNA sequences and specific genes are defective in all tumor cells. Moreover, every tumor starts with one mutated cell, the offspring of which are also mutated. A single mutation does not give rise to cancer; several mutations are required. The development of a tumor is a multistep process. Transforming cells accumulate several mutations before they become fully malignant.

Most human cancer cells not only contain lots of mutations, but they are also genetically unstable. That is, the cells continue to add to their collection of genetic errors at an ever-increasing rate. The reason for this increased rate of error is that some mutations can directly interfere with the normally accurate replication of DNA. In addition, some mutations interfere with the repair of DNA errors.

Even during normal DNA replication in a healthy cell, mistakes occur. Sometimes DNA can be damaged in a healthy cell, just as it is in a cancer cell. Ordinarily, DNA repair mechanisms that exist in cells can fix these mistakes and small bits of damage. However, if a cell acquires a mutation in a gene that is needed for DNA repair, DNA damage or replication errors won't be fixed in that cell. As a consequence, other mutations that occur will also not be repaired and the rate of error accumulation can increase dramatically. Cells that can't repair DNA errors are especially vulnerable to becoming cancerous because they have a greater chance of experiencing a cancer-causing mutation that also won't be repaired.

Finally, some mutations involve large-scale damage to the structure of chromosomes. Chromosomes are composed of DNA and protein and are the components of the cell where the genes or information for inheritance are found. Pieces of a chromosome may break off and get lost or get stuck back on another chromosome in an abnormal way. When this occurs, lots of genes can be lost or be put some place where they are not properly regulated. Even the cell's best DNA repair mechanisms cannot fix these large structural problems in chromosomes.

SUMMARY

The study of tumor viruses led to the discovery of oncogenes, or genes that cause cancer. Oncogenes originate from normal cellular proto-oncogenes that have mutated. Tumor suppressor genes are important for regulating cell proliferation. When they are damaged, cancer usually results. The inability of a cell to repair DNA or chromosome damage also increases the likelihood of tumor formation.

3

ONCOGENES

KEY POINTS

♦ Experiments have confirmed that oncogenes originate from cellular proto-oncogenes.

♦ Proto-oncogenes encode for proteins important for normal cell behaviors such as proliferation, differentiation, and survival.

♦ Proto-oncogenes can be converted to oncogenes by a change in gene structure, location, or function. Oncogenes overstimulate cell proliferation.

WHERE DO ONCOGENES COME FROM?

Starting with Peyton Rous's discovery of tumor viruses in 1911, followed by research done in the 1970s that proved that cancer genes exist, people wondered where cancer genes originate. The notion that our DNA has genes that can go haywire and cause cancer seemed far-fetched to many scientists. Even Peyton Rous, in his 1966 Nobel Prize address, argued strongly against a role for a cell's own genes in the development of cancer. Also in 1966, Dr. Robert Huebner and Dr. George Todaro proposed the Oncogene Hypothesis, which stated that oncogenes had been introduced into vertebrate groups by viruses millions of years ago. They suggested that these oncogenes remained silent unless activated by a carcinogen. An alternate explanation for the origin of oncogenes, mentioned in Chapter 2, was that they started out as normal cellular genes that got trapped inside viruses and, hence, made that virus **tumorigenic** like RSV.

Which of these two possible scenarios is correct has actually been determined through experimentation. Scientists infected 150 mice with a nontransforming virus, one that could not, by itself, cause cancer. Out of this population of mice, one unlucky mouse developed **lymphoma**, a cancer of the immune system. Next, scientists isolated a virus from the lymphoma cells and found that the virus now contained an oncogene. Evidently, the virus had picked up a gene from the lymphoma cell. Further analysis identified this oncogene as *abl*. This experiment was very important, because it showed that, once in a while, a host cell gene will be incorporated into a virus and go on to produce an oncogenic virus. Finally, analysis of normal cells showed that *abl* is indeed a normal cellular gene. These results show that although Huebner and Todaro's Oncogene Hypothesis did help encourage research, it was ultimately not correct. The demonstration that viruses could take over normal cellular genes was strong evidence to support the hypothesis that oncogenes had a cellular and not a viral origin.

HOW DO NORMAL CELLULAR GENES BECOME ONCOGENIC?

Given that some normal cellular genes have the capacity to operate abnormally and transform cells into cancer, it's important to look at

SPOTLIGHT ON CANCER SCIENTISTS

J. MICHAEL BISHOP (1936–   )

When J. Michael Bishop was a high school student, he took a career aptitude test that predicted he would have a career as a journalist, forester, or music teacher. There was no suggestion of a future in biomedical research. Obviously, the aptitude test was not completely accurate; Bishop won the 1989 Nobel Prize in Physiology or Medicine, jointly with Harold Varmus, for their work showing that cells have normal genes that can be altered to become oncogenes and thus contribute to the development of cancer.

Born in 1936 in York, Pennsylvania, Bishop obtained his early education in a two-room schoolhouse where the curriculum lacked much mention of science. Bishop then attended a small high school; there were only 80 students in his graduating class. Because of the influence of his family physician, Bishop decided he wanted to go to medical school. He attended Gettysburg College, completed a major in chemistry, and was accepted to Harvard Medical School, where he intended to prepare for a career in

Figure 3.1 Co-recipient of the 1989 Nobel prize, J. Michael Bishop conducted groundbreaking research into the viruses that cause cancer. (*NIH/NLM*)

academic medicine. Unfortunately, Bishop quickly realized that the way to become a professor in biomedicine was through research, not teaching—compared to his classmates, Bishop was poorly prepared to do research. In fact, when he applied for a summer job in a neurobiology lab, he was turned down because he lacked research experience. Bishop wondered whether he should even return to medical school. Recognizing his talent and ambition, a professor in the pathology department rescued Bishop with an offer of a year's independent study in a research laboratory. After this experience, Bishop renewed his medical studies and began to study animal viruses. At first, the research was part-time, but eventually the dean of the medical school allowed Bishop to forego most of the required fourth-year medical curriculum and instead work full-time on his research.

After he graduated from medical school and worked as a resident for two years at Massachusetts General Hospital, Bishop finally got the focused research training he wanted. He entered the Research Associate Training Program at the National Institutes of Health (NIH). This program was designed to train physicians in basic research. Bishop spent several years at the NIH and, in 1968, he accepted a faculty position at the University of California, San Francisco (UCSF). There, he studied animal viruses, including those that cause cancer. He has also done groundbreaking work on cancer-causing genes and how they function, doing a great deal of his research in collaboration with Harold Varmus. Although Bishop is most famous for his research, he has always felt that his work as a teacher has been an equally important part of his career. He continued to both research and teach until 1998 at UCSF, where he is now chancellor of the university.

how these cellular genes, or proto-oncogenes, function under healthy conditions. After all, proto-oncogenes certainly don't reside in cells like ticking time bombs just waiting for an opportunity to cause cancer. In fact, proto-oncogenes all code for proteins that are essential for some aspect of cell proliferation, survival, or differentiation. For example, some proteins encoded by proto-oncogenes are part of cell communication pathways and act as growth factors. Others are cell membrane receptors that receive these growth signals. Some are signal molecules inside a cell that relay the information gathered at the cell surface, where receptors bind to growth factor molecules, to sites inside the cell and its nucleus. Some proteins even bind directly to DNA to turn gene expression on and off, meaning that they regulate whether or not particular genes direct the production of specific proteins. All of these proteins function together in a complex pathway that regulates cell division.

Because proteins encoded by certain proto-oncogenes can regulate cell division, it makes sense that if one or more of these genes were altered, then the proteins they encode could become faulty and cell proliferation could be stuck in the "on" position. In other words, proto-oncogenes can be changed into oncogenes, which, if present in cells, can cause cancer. This leads us to the question: How do proto-oncogenes become oncogenes?

In all cases, proto-oncogenes are transformed into oncogenes because of a change in gene structure, location, or function, which results in an overproduction of protein or the production of an overactive, unregulated protein. See Table 3.1. There are specific types of genetic changes that can turn an oncogene into a proto-oncogene. First, a mutation in which just one of the four letters (A, T, G, C) of the genetic code of the DNA, is changed to a different letter (A to G, for example) can result in the synthesis of an altered protein. Such an alteration would be like changing the letter

TABLE 3.1	SOME EXAMPLES OF ONCOGENES GROUPED TOGETHER BY PROTEIN FORMATIONS		
ONCOGENE NAME	PROTEIN PRODUCED	ONCOGENE ORIGIN	COMMON CANCER TYPE*
1. Growth Factors			
v-sis	PDGF	Viral	Sarcomas (monkeys)
COLIA1-PDGFB	PDGF	Translocation	Fibrosarcoma
2. Receptors			
v-erb-b	EGF receptor	Viral	Leukemia (chickens)
TRK	Nerve growth factor receptor	DNA rearrangement	Thyroid
ERBB2	ErbB2 receptor	Amplification	Breast
v-mpl	Thrombopoietin receptor	Viral	Leukemia (mice)
3. Plasma membrane GTP-binding proteins			
KRAS	Ras	Point mutation	Pancreas, colon, lung, others
HRAS	Ras	Point mutation	Bladder
NRAS	Ras	Point mutation	Leukemia
4. Nonreceptor protein kinases			
BRAF	Raf kinase	Point mutation	Melanoma
v-src	Src kinase	Viral	Sarcomas (chickens)

(continues)

TABLE 3.1 SOME EXAMPLES OF ONCOGENES GROUPED TOGETHER BY PROTEIN FORMATIONS (continued)			
ONCOGENE NAME	PROTEIN PRODUCED	ONCOGENE ORIGIN	COMMON CANCER TYPE*
SRC	Src kinase	DNA rearrangement	Colon
TEL-JAK2	Jak kinase	Translocation	Leukemias
BCR-ABL	Abl kinase	Translocation	Chronic myelogenous leukemia
5. Transcription factors			
MYC	Myc	Translocation	Burkitt's lymphoma
MYCL	Myc	Amplification	Small cell lung cancer
c-myc	Myc	Insertional mutagenesis	Leukemia (chickens)
v-jun	Jun	Viral	Sarcomas (chickens)
v-fos	Fos	Viral	Bone (mice)
6. Cell-cycle or cell-death regulators			
CYCD1	Cyclin	Amplification, translocation	Breast, lymphoma
CDK4	Cdk	Amplification	Sarcoma, glioblastoma
BCL2	Bcl-2	Translocation	Non-Hodgkins lymphoma

* Cancers are in humans unless otherwise specified. Only the most frequent cancer types are listed.

Source: Becker, Wayne M., Lewis J. Kleinsmith, and Jeff Hardin. *The World of the Cell*, 6th ed. San Francisco: Pearson Education/Benjamin Cummings, 2006, p. 779.

of a word to a different one—for example, "cat" into "*bat*"—thus changing the meaning entirely. A change in one letter of the DNA code is referred to as a **point mutation**. The oncogene *ras* is an example of an oncogene produced by a single change in the DNA sequence of the gene.

Second, genes can sometimes undergo **amplification**. This means that they make copies of themselves and insert these copies into the cell's own chromosomes. As a result, a cell could have so many copies of a proto-oncogene that too much protein is produced and oncogenic behavior results even though the structure of the proto-oncogene is normal. The oncogene *N-myc* is an example of a proto-oncogene that, when amplified, becomes oncogenic.

Third, chromosomes can break and rearrange their pieces. If a proto-oncogene is moved to a new location on the chromosome, it may be un-regulated and may get stuck in the "on" position so that it behaves as an oncogene. The movement, or **translocation**, of *c-myc* makes it oncogenic.

As mentioned in Chapter 2, scientists have identified at least 100 onco-genes. All of them originated as normal cellular proto-oncogenes. Some are found as oncogenes in tumor viruses, but most proto-oncogenes that become oncogenic do so without ever having entered a virus. The proto-oncogenes always code for a particular protein that is important for the regulation of cell proliferation or survival. For all of the proto-oncogenes, transformation to an oncogene also entails some type of change or altera-tion in gene structure, location, or function. See Table 3.2.

Let's take a closer look at several examples of specific oncogenes in order to understand this category of cancer genes more fully.

Src Oncogene

As described in Chapter 2, *src* was the first oncogene identified, initially in the Rous sarcoma virus (RSV). Ultimately, *src* was shown to be part of the normal cellular genome. The *src* oncogene forms as a result of a

TABLE 3.2 REPRESENTATIVE ONCOGENES OF HUMAN TUMORS

Oncogene	Type of Cancer	Activation Mechanism
abl	Chronic myeloid leukemia, acute lymphocytic leukemia	Translocation
akt	Breast, ovarian, and pancreatic carcinomas	Amplification
bcl-2	Follicular B-cell lymphoma	Translocation
D1	Parathyroid adenoma, B-cell lymphoma	Translocation
D1	Squamous cell, bladder, breast, esophageal, liver, and lung carcinomas	Amplification
E2A/pbx1	Acute lymphocytic leukemia	Translocation
erbB-2	Breast and ovarian carcinomas	Amplification
Gip	Adrenal cortical and ovarian carcinomas	Point mutation
Gli	Glioblastoma	Amplification
Gsp	Pituitary and thyroid tumors	Point mutation
hox-11	Acute T-cell leukemia	Translocation
lyl	Acute T-cell leukemia	Translocation
c-myc	Burkitt's lymphoma	Translocation
c-myc	Breast and lung carcinoma	Amplification
L-myc	Lung carcinoma	Amplification
N-myc	Neuroblastoma, lung carcinoma	Amplification

Oncogene	Type of Cancer	Activation Mechanism
PDGFR	Chronic myelomonocytic leukemia	Translocation
P13K	Ovarian carcinoma	Amplification
PML/RARα	Acute promyelocytic leukemia	Translocation
B-raf	Melanoma, colon carcinoma	Point mutation
rasH	Thyroid carcinoma	Point mutation
rasK	Colon, lung, pancreatic, and thyroid carcinomas	Point mutation
rasN	Acute myeloid and lymphocytic leukemias, thyroid carcinoma	Point mutation
ret	Multiple endocrine neoplasia types 2A and 2B	Point mutation
ret	Thyroid carcinoma	DNA rearrangement
SMO	Basal cell carcinoma	Point mutation

Source: Cooper, Geoffrey M. and Robert E. Hausman. *The Cell: A Molecular Approach*, 3rd ed. Washington, DC: ASM Press, 2004, p. 650.

point mutation in the *src* proto-oncogene that is found in normal cells. Specifically, one **nucleotide** was changed in the DNA of the *src* gene, resulting in one **amino acid** being changed in the protein that the gene encodes. The specific protein the *src* gene encodes is called tyrosine kinase. Under normal circumstances, tyrosine kinase helps regulate cell proliferation. The job of tyrosine kinase is to add a phosphate (a chemical group) to other molecules, thus activating them. These activated molecules then regulate other molecules whose actions eventually cause cells to divide. When *src* is in its oncogenic form, the altered tyrosine kinase gets turned on permanently, adding phosphates to other molecules in the signal pathway and activating them continuously. As a result, the cell-signaling pathway gets stuck "on" and unregulated cell

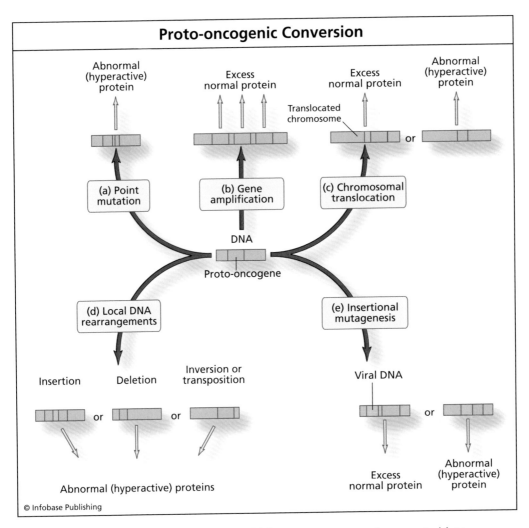

© Infobase Publishing

Figure 3.2 There are several methods by which a proto-oncogene is converted into an oncogene.

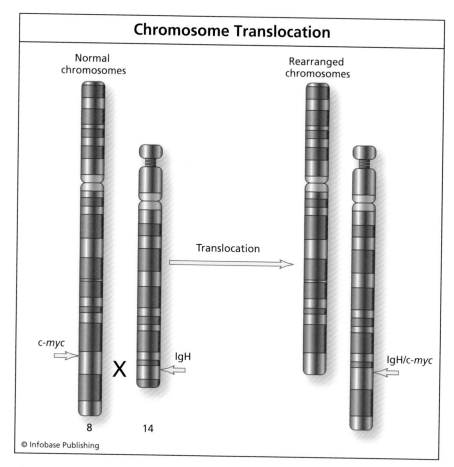

Figure 3.3 Movement of the proto-oncogene *c-myc* from one chromosme to a specific location on another, a process called translocation, leads to Burkitt's lymphoma.

division occurs. In this particular scenario, the type of cancer that forms is a sarcoma, a tumor of connective tissue and muscle.

Ras Oncogene

Found in tumor cells in 20 percent of all human cancers, 25 percent of lung cancers, and 50 percent of colon cancers, the *ras* oncogene is a major cancer-causing gene. Like *src*, *ras* becomes an oncogene because

SPOTLIGHT ON CANCER SCIENTISTS
HAROLD E. VARMUS (1939–)

Of the many honors awarded to cancer scientist Harold Varmus, two stand out: the 1989 Nobel Prize for Physiology or Medicine that he shared with J. Michael Bishop and the invitation to throw out the first pitch of the 1990 baseball season for the San Francisco Giants. Varmus threw a perfect strike.

Varmus is the grandson of immigrants who originally came from Austria and Poland. Because of the hard work of his grandparents, Varmus's mother and father were able to get excellent educations. His father attended Harvard College and got his medical degree from Tufts; his mother attended Wellesley College and the New York School of Social Work. Like his parents, Varmus received a first-class education.

When he started at Amherst College in 1957, Varmus planned to go on to medical school; however, his focus shifted to philosophy and English literature. Upon graduation, he was awarded a fellowship to study literature at Harvard, but his interest in medicine returned and he began his studies at Columbia University's College of Physicians and Surgeons. At first, he intended to specialize in psychiatry and international medicine, but eventually Varmus became more attracted to medical research.

of a point mutation of the *ras* proto-oncogene. The protein encoded by *ras* is also part of the cell-signaling pathway that regulates cell proliferation. The protein that *ras* encodes serves the function of telling the cell that a signal outside the cell, such as a growth factor, has bound to a receptor molecule on the cell membrane. The normal *ras* protein

Varmus completed his medical degree in 1966. He then worked in a hospital in India and as a resident physician at Columbia-Presbyterian Hospital. Then, he joined a research lab at the National Institutes of Health (NIH) to get training in research. He decided to continue his research in the study of tumor viruses and joined J. Michael Bishop's lab as a postdoctoral fellow in 1970. From then on, Varmus and Bishop worked in close collaboration on the issue of cancer-causing genes. After jointly receiving the Nobel Prize with Bishop in 1989, Varmus moved on enthusiastically to a new challenge. He became the first Nobel laureate ever appointed to direct the NIH. He held this important position until 2000. Since then, Varmus has been the president of Memorial Sloan-Kettering in New York City, one of the most prestigious cancer hospitals and research centers in the world.

Figure 3.4   After co-winning the Nobel prize in 1989 Harold E. Varmus went on to lead the National Institutes of Health. (*NIH/NLM*)

"notices" this binding between the growth factor and the receptor and then activates other signal molecules inside the cell, telling the cell to divide. When *ras* is oncogenic, the protein it encodes activates signal molecules inside the cell, even if it has not detected the binding of a growth factor to a receptor. As a consequence, cell division is triggered even if no growth factors are present. The result of this unregulated cell division may be a tumor if nothing stops the process.

C-myc Oncogene

Produced by the movement, or translocation, of the *c-myc* proto-oncogene from one chromosome to a specific location on another chromosome, the *c-myc* oncogene contributes to the development of Burkitt's lymphoma, which is a cancer of the immune system. The movement of the *c-myc* gene to its new location removes the normal controls of the gene's expression. The function of the normal *c-myc* protein is to bind to DNA and regulate gene expression for a pathway that stimulates cell division. In other words, *c-myc* controls whether the genes that direct the production of proteins necessary for making cells divide are active or not. When it is moved to a new location, the *c-myc* oncogene functions in an unregulated manner and causes the production of an abnormally high amount of the *c-myc* protein. Because so much *c-myc* protein is produced from the oncogene, cell proliferation is overstimulated and cancer results.

ONCOGENES AND THE REGULATION OF CELL DIVISION

The 100-or-so oncogenes that have been discovered come from normal genes that play important roles in cell proliferation and survival. Some specific examples of oncogenes that function at the various steps of this "relay" pathway illustrate how oncogenes relate to the normal function of cell regulation. First, cells need growth factors to stimulate cell division. When it is active, the oncogene *sis* encodes a growth factor that is made continuously. As a consequence, cells with an active *sis* oncogene actually secrete the very growth factor that triggers their own proliferation—they stimulate their own cell division.

Second, growth factors need to bind to cell surface receptors so that the communication pathway will continue. The oncogene *erb-B* encodes for an abnormal version of a growth factor receptor. This dysfunctional receptor behaves as if the growth factor is bound all the time, even if no factor is actually present.

Third, after growth factors and receptors bind, molecules inside the cell continue the communication pathway. As previously described, the *src* and *ras* oncogenes produce abnormal versions of intracellular signal molecules that activate other molecules in the pathway, even when they have not been told to do so. Eventually, the signal from the pathway will reach the chromosomes, and gene expression will be affected. The oncogenes *c-myc* and *c-fos* produce transcription factors, which are molecules that bind directly to DNA and regulate gene function. In the cases of *c-myc* and *c-fos*, these transcription factors overstimulate

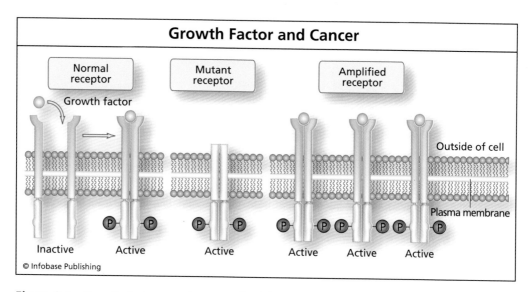

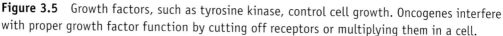

Figure 3.5 Growth factors, such as tyrosine kinase, control cell growth. Oncogenes interfere with proper growth factor function by cutting off receptors or multiplying them in a cell.

gene expression and result in too much proliferation. Finally, cells live in a delicate balance between dividing to make new cells or dying. The oncogene *bcl-1* codes for a protein that blocks cell suicide. When *bcl-1* is active, damaged cells that ought to undergo apoptosis fail to do so and instead continue to divide, producing a population of defective cells.

Proto-oncogenes play a critical role in the regulation of cell proliferation. When they become oncogenes and function abnormally, cell division is overstimulated. The next chapter will consider the other major category of cancer genes: tumor suppressors. These genes normally play the role of putting the brakes on cell division but can lead to cancer when they fail to do their job properly.

SUMMARY

Although there are tumor-causing viruses, the genes that trigger cancer development actually originate in cells as proto-oncogenes. Encoding proteins that are essential for normal cell behaviors, including proliferation, proto-oncogenes can be converted to oncogenes through a change in their structure, chromosomal location, or function. When oncogenes are activated, cell division occurs in an uncontrolled manner, leading to cancer.

4

TUMOR SUPPRESSORS

KEY POINTS

- Tumor suppressor genes encode for proteins that regulate cell survival and slow or stop cell proliferation.

- When tumor suppressor genes are mutated, the normal inhibition of cell division does not occur, and abnormal cells ignore signals that direct them to die.

- Mutated tumor suppressor genes are associated with most types of cancer.

- Inheritance of a mutated tumor suppressor gene increases the likelihood of cancer.

LI-FRAUMENI SYNDROME

In 1969, Frederick Li and Joseph Fraumeni described several families with unusual and startling patterns of cancer. In one of the families, the initial patient was a three-year-old child who had developed a soft-tissue sarcoma, which is a type of tumor found in tissue such as muscle. This child's sister developed a soft-tissue sarcoma by the time she was one year old. The children's mother had breast cancer at the age of 22 and, by age 34, she had cancer in the other breast, as well as a thyroid tumor. A first cousin of the two children developed **leukemia** by age five, their aunt was diagnosed with breast cancer when she was 32, and their grandfather had pancreatic cancer. Li and Fraumeni had discovered a rare cancer pattern, now called Li-Fraumeni syndrome (LFS). LFS is characterized by its heritability, the early onset of tumors in affected individuals, the variety in the types of cancers that develop, and the appearance of multiple primary tumors—often in different tissues—in the same person. While cancer can spread, or metastasize, to produce new tumors in an individual, in LFS, each tumor is a new and independent event—not the result of an invasion from another tumor elsewhere in the body.

LFS is a relatively rare disorder. Only around 400 families have been diagnosed with LFS worldwide. The most prevalent types of tumors that occur in individuals with this disorder are soft tissue **carcinoma**, **osteosarcoma**, breast cancer, brain tumors, leukemia, and cancer of the adrenal gland. LFS is also associated with increased incidences of cancers of the stomach, ovary, colon, rectum, endometrium, thyroid, pancreas, prostate, cervix, and melanoma. What could possibly account for the inheritance patterns observed with LFS, as well as the wide variety of cancers that develop?

TUMOR SUPPRESSORS AND LFS

There are two categories of genes involved in the development of cancer: oncogenes and tumor suppressor genes. To discover which specific genes are involved in the production of a tumor, the genes in tumor cells must be compared to those in normal cells.

When **sporadic**, or nonhereditary, brain tumors, lung tumors, soft-tissue sarcomas, osteosarcomas, and leukemias were analyzed, they all showed a mutation in the tumor suppressor gene *p53*. Other studies showed that mice with mutant *p53* genes had an increased incidence of osteosarcomas, soft-tissue sarcomas, adrenal gland tumors, and lung cancer. These mice were developing the same types of tumors seen in human LFS patients. Scientists looked at the results of both of these studies and decided to examine people with LFS to determine whether their *p53* gene is mutated. They found out that it is. Individuals with LFS inherit a mutated form of *p53* in every cell of their entire body. As is the case with

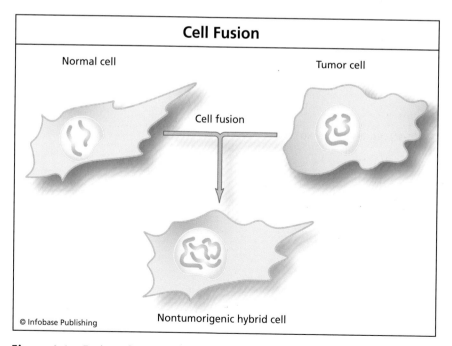

Figure 4.1 Fusion of a normal cell with a cancer cell initially produces a nontumorigenic hybrid cell, which results in suppression of tumorigenicity.

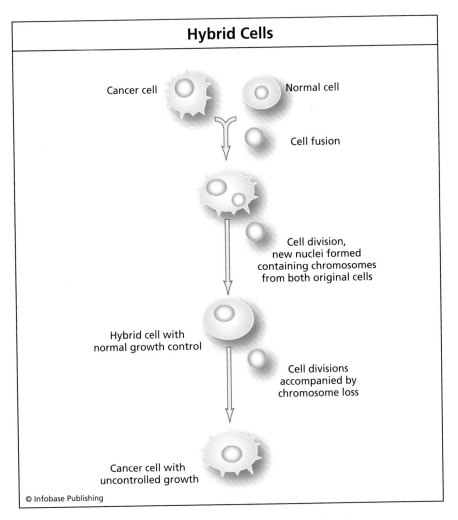

Hybrid Cells

Cancer cell

Normal cell

Cell fusion

Cell division,
new nuclei formed
containing chromosomes
from both original cells

Hybrid cell with
normal growth control

Cell divisions
accompanied by
chromosome loss

Cancer cell with
uncontrolled growth

© Infobase Publishing

Figure 4.2 As nontumorigenic hybrid cells divide over time, chromosomes are lost, tumor suppression fails, and uncontrolled, or cancerous, cell growth occurs.

all genes, each person has two copies of *p53*—one inherited from the mother and one from the father. If the second copy of *p53* were damaged or faulty, the individual would lack the *p53* tumor suppressor protein. As a consequence, the likelihood that cancer would develop somewhere, or even in multiple places, would increase dramatically. In LFS families, the probability that an individual will develop an invasive cancer by the age of 30 is 50 percent, whereas the probability is only 1 percent among the general population. By age 70, more than 90 percent of individuals who inherited a mutated *p53* will exhibit LFS and develop cancer.

WHAT DO TUMOR SUPPRESSORS DO?

Whereas oncogene activity generally directs cells to continue cell division, even when it is inappropriate, mutated or damaged tumor suppressor genes fail to stop cell proliferation. Functional tumor suppressor genes encode for proteins that control whether or not cells will survive and, if they do survive, whether they will reproduce. Although there are approximately 30,000 genes in each human cell, only a few dozen of them encode tumor suppressors. Nevertheless, losing just one of these functional tumor suppressor genes can have very serious health consequences. Tumor suppressor genes can be considered "gatekeepers" because their loss opens the gate to excessive cell proliferation. In addition to gatekeeper genes, there are also "caretaker" genes that are important for DNA repair and the normal sorting of chromosomes during cell division. The caretaker genes are essential for maintaining genetic stability, but they don't actually control cell proliferation.

There are a variety of ways that tumor suppressor genes exert their influence on cells. The proteins encoded by tumor suppressor genes can be divided into four functional categories. First, there are proteins inside the cell that inhibit the progression of cells through a particular stage of the cycle of cell growth and division. In other words, these proteins stop cell division from occurring by preventing the necessary events for division that occur inside the cell. Second, some proteins act as receptors that bind hormones or chemical signals that tell the cell not to divide. Third, there are proteins that stop cell division if the DNA has been damaged, or if chromosomes are abnormal. Finally, there are proteins that will trigger apoptosis, or "cell suicide," if DNA or chromosome damage is too severe to repair. In all cases, the proteins made by tumor suppressor genes evaluate some aspect of whether cells should be able to divide and/or survive.

The *p53* Supressor Gene

The most important tumor suppressor by far is *p53*, which is encoded by the *p53* gene. This tumor suppressor is mutated, or lost, in 50 percent of all human tumors, including both inherited and noninherited forms. The control pathway, which includes *p53*, causes cells either to stop dividing or to die by apoptosis in the event that DNA is badly damaged. In addition to random mutation or cellular accidents, there are many events and molecules that influence the *p53* protein. For example, *p53* is inactivated by the oncogenic proteins produced by several types of tumor viruses, such as SV40, adenovirus, human papillomavirus, and Kaposi's sarcoma–associated herpes virus. Tobacco carcinogens also produce point mutations in the *p53* genes of cells in lung tumors, while sunlight produces mutations in the *p53* genes of skin cancer cells.

Although the role of *p53* protein as a tumor suppressor is critical, this is only one reason it is important in cells. As components of an overall response pathway for cellular stress (meaning that the cell or parts of the cell become damaged or nonfunctional) *p53* genes are activated by many problems, such as DNA damage, **hypoxia**, nucleotide imbalance, and damage to the **mitotic spindle**. The *p53* protein governs the cell's protective responses to these challenges. Specifically, *p53* protein, along with some other molecules, can assess the degree of damage that has been done to the DNA and chromosomes.

The *p53* protein is actually a transcription factor—a molecule that regulates whether other genes are active. When genes are active, they direct the production of other proteins. If genes are turned off and therefore inactive, no proteins are made. When the DNA is damaged, *p53* regulates the genes that are involved in repairing it, controlling cell divi-

TABLE 4.1 EXAMPLES OF HUMAN TUMOR SUPPRESSOR GENES		
GENE	INHERITED SYNDROME	CANCER TYPE
APC	Familial adenomatous polyposis	Colon
BRCA1	Familial breast cancer	Breast, ovary
BRCA2	Familial breast cancer	Breast
SMAD4	Colorectal cancer	Colon, rectal
NF-1	Neurofibromatosis type 1	Neurofibromas
NF-2	Neurofibromatosis type 2	Schwann cells, meninges
CDKN2A	Familial melanoma	Melanoma, others
p53	Li-Fraumeni	Bone, breast, leukemia, brain, adrenal, others
RB	Hereditary retinoblastoma	Retina, bone, others
HL	Von Hippel-Lindau	Kidney, retina, brain
WT-1	Wilms' tumor	Kidney

Source: Becker, M. Wayne, Lewis J. Kleinsmith, and Jeff Hardin. *The World of the Cell,* 6th ed. Pearson/ Benjamin Cummings: San Francisco, 2006, p. 784

sion, and directing apoptosis. If the degree of damage is not too severe, *p53* halts the cell growth and division cycle and directs the repair of the damage. If there is too much damage, *p53* induces apoptosis.

SPOTLIGHT ON CANCER SCIENTISTS
SIR HENRY HARRIS (1925-)

Figure 4.3 Sir Henry Harris demonstrated the existence of tumor suppressor gene behavior. His research was the foundation of somatic cell genetics, the mapping of genes in human chromosomes, and the development of monoclonal antibody technology. *(Michael Noakes)*

The origins of Henry Harris's interest in medicine and biomedical research may seem a little unusual. Born in 1925 in Australia, Harris actually began his studies in modern languages. It was through his literary interests that Harris first became attracted to medicine. Rather than continue his education in literature, Harris chose to study medicine at the Royal Prince Albert Hospital. After earning his medical degree, he began a career in research.

Harris moved to England in the early 1950s and earned his doctoral degree at the Sir William Dunn School of Pathology, Oxford University. He then settled into a very productive research career. By 1964, he was appointed head of the Dunn School

Given the importance of genetic stability for the normal regulation and functioning of cell division, it is easy to see how knocking out *p53*'s function could result in uncontrolled cell proliferation and the

of Pathology. In 1979, he was appointed to one of the most prestigious positions in the biomedical field, the Regius Professor of Medicine at Oxford.

People usually make major career advances in science because of important research breakthroughs and discoveries. While Harris made essential contributions to cancer research by demonstrating the existence of tumor suppressor gene behavior (as discussed in Chapter 2), his cell fusion research was the foundation of **somatic cell genetics,** which is a technique to figure out the function of specific genes. Somatic cell genetics is also used for the **mapping** of the physical location of specific genes in human chromosomes, as well as the development of **monoclonal antibody** technology. Monoclonal antibodies are made by specially fused and cultured cells of the immune system. The monoclonal antibodies that these cells produce are very specific and can be used to study, and even treat, some types of cancer cells.

Now in retirement, Harris continues to work on the problem of cancer, challenging his fellow researchers to focus on cancer not just as a disorder in which cell proliferation is unregulated, but as a condition in which cell differentiation is improperly controlled. Because cells fail to specialize, they continue to divide instead. According to this view, the functions of oncogenes and tumor suppressor genes need to be reevaluated to consider what roles these genes play in regulating cell differentiation as well as cell proliferation.

development of a tumor. It is also evident how the inheritance of a mutated *p53* gene, as seen with LFS, makes a person vulnerable to cancer at any age and with almost any body tissue.

OTHER TUMOR SUPPRESSOR GENES

Approximately 70 percent of all people with LFS have inherited a mutant *p53* gene. In fact, the majority of heritable cancers involve a tumor suppressor mutation. For example, inherited breast cancer is caused by mutated *BRCA1* and *BRCA2* genes. These genes encode for proteins that are important for regulating DNA repair and cell division. Similarly, another tumor suppressor gene, *RB*, encodes a protein that can stop the cell division cycle. Inheritance of mutated *RB* often leads to **retinoblastoma**, a cancer of the retina in the eye. Inherited mutations in the tumor suppressor *APC* can lead to the development of colon cancer.

Although mutated tumor suppressor genes are implicated in several types of inherited cancer, they are also evident in nonhereditary cancers. Defective *p53* protein has been observed in 50 percent of all human tumors. Other tumor suppressors also play important roles in the development of particular cancers. For example, the *DPC4* gene is inactivated in some pancreatic cancers. As a consequence, the protein it encodes, which normally inhibits cell proliferation, is absent and a tumor forms.

It is interesting to note that the normal protein products of proto-oncogenes enhance cell division, while those of normal tumor suppressors inhibit the same process. In many cases, there is an activating protein and an inhibitory protein that operate on the exact same step of the pathway. For instance, in certain types of leukemia and nervous system cancers, the tumor suppressor gene *NF-1* is mutated. Ordinarily, normal *NF-1* inhibits the function of the protein that is encoded by the proto-oncogene *ras*. The normal *ras* protein activates cell division. When the *NF-1* protein is defective, it does not stop the *ras* protein from triggering cell division and uncontrolled cell proliferation results. Table 4.1 on page 57 provides examples of human tumor supressor genes.

Sometimes the balancing act between the activators and inhibitors of cell division can be quite complex. The chemical signal *TGF-β* is produced by normal cells and stops cell division in several types of cells. In some colon cancer cells, the *TGF-β* signal to stop cell division is ignored because the cancer cells have a mutated form of the gene that codes for the receptor for the *TGF-β* signal. As a consequence, the receptor does not function and cell division continues. Even when the *TGF-β* signal binds to a normal receptor, other steps in the regulatory pathway can still go wrong. Under normal circumstances, *TGF-β* shuts down cell division through the action of another protein, called *p15*. In some cancers, the *p15* protein is missing. Therefore, the signal to stop cell division is not passed on successfully. As you can see, the decision about whether cells should live and divide is made as a result of an elaborate dance between activating molecules that are encoded by proto-oncogenes and inhibitory molecules that are encoded by tumor suppressors.

SUMMARY

Tumor suppressor genes are responsible for directing the production of proteins that regulate cell survival and proliferation. Whereas the proteins encoded by proto-oncogenes generally activate proliferation and enhance cell survival, tumor suppressor proteins slow or stop cell division and trigger the destruction of defective cells. When tumor suppressor genes are mutated, these inhibitory controls are lost. Uncontrolled cell division and cancer result.

5

CHROMOSOMAL ABNORMALITIES AND CANCER

KEY POINTS

- Chromosomes contain genes.

- Many types of chromosome damage cannot be repaired, and lost chromosomes cannot be retrieved.

- Some types of chromosomal abnormalities can result in cancer because genes are unable to function normally.

- Some cancers are associated with specific chromosomal defects.

- Telomeres are special stabilizing structures found at the ends of chromosomes.

- In most human cells, telomeres shorten with each cell division. Cells die when the telomeres get too short.

> ♦ In most cancer cells, telomerase is activated and telomere short-ening is prevented, thus immortalizing the cells.
>
> ♦ Genetic instability increases the likelihood of cancer.

CHROMOSOMES

Cancer is a genetic disease in the sense that alterations in specific genes, particularly proto-oncogenes and tumor suppressor genes, can lead to the formation of tumors. Although small genetic changes can produce oncogenic mutations, large changes that involve chromosomes—the structures within cells that contain genes in linear DNA molecules—can also result in cancer. Unlike small genetic flaws that sometimes can be repaired by replacing the incorrect base (A, T, G, or C) with the correct one, the alteration of chromosome structure or mistakes in the numbers of chromosomes in a cell cannot be fixed. Cells that have these types of errors are destined to keep them as long as they live and to pass them on to their offspring cells.

TYPES OF CHROMOSOME DAMAGE

Each cell of the human body contains 46 chromosomes: a set of 23 inher-ited from the mother and a set of 23 inherited from the father. Only the sex cells—the eggs or sperm—have a different number: just one complete set of 23 chromosomes per cell. When the somatic or non-sex cells of the human body divide, they produce new cells. Each one contains a full set of 46 chromosomes. Sometimes things go wrong during cell division, and chromosomes can be broken, lost, or left behind. When these events occur, the resulting cells may have extra chromosomes, chromosomes that are missing pieces, chromosomes that break and then reconnect the pieces incorrectly, or they may even be missing some chromosomes entirely. Cells need to have complete, normal chromosomes present in the correct numbers to properly balance the activities of genes. When this delicately regulated situation breaks down due to chromosomal abnormalities, uncontrolled cell division and cancer can occur.

HOW DO WE KNOW THAT CHROMOSOME DAMAGE CAN LEAD TO CANCER?

In the early 1900s, German scientist Theodor Boveri did some experiments in which he managed to have more than one sea urchin sperm fuse with a single sea urchin egg. Ordinarily, sea urchin fertilization, like that of other organisms, entails the fusion of one sperm and one egg. Boveri carefully studied the polyspermic eggs he created and followed the behavior of the chromosomes. He observed that the abnormal number of chromosomes that resulted from the fusion of multiple sperm with one egg produced abnormal cell division. He also noted that the type of structure that developed depended upon which specific chromosomes were present in a particular embryo.

These observations led Boveri to propose that chromosomes carried heritable information. He went even further and cited descriptions of chromosomal abnormalities in cancer cells made by Dr. David von Hansemann in 1890. Boveri then speculated that cancer might be caused by chromosomal abnormalities, especially extra or missing chromosomes in individual cells. At first, no one paid much attention to Boveri's idea—after all, he was making an amazing leap from sea urchins to human cancer. Nevertheless, Boveri expanded his ideas about the relationship between chromosomes and cancer, and in 1914 he published *The Origin of Malignant Tumors.* This book was a very important and respected contribution to medical literature. Long before anyone knew anything about the physical structure of genes, how they function, or even DNA, Boveri was able to determine that cancer was a genetic disease. As Boveri wrote,

> The unlimited tendency to rapid proliferation in malignant tumor cells [could result] from a permanent predominance of the chromosomes that promote division. . . . Another possibility [to explain cancer] is the presence of definite chromosomes which inhibit division. . . . Cells of tumors with unlimited growth would arise if those "inhibiting chromosomes" were eliminated . . . . [Because] each kind of chromosome is represented twice in the normal cell, the depression of only one of these two might pass unnoticed.[2]

Because Boveri's ideas were ahead of their time, the techniques and tools necessary to study chromosome function in detail were not yet available. How did scientists bridge the gap between Boveri's theory and the present-day understanding of the relationship between chromosomes and cancer? What scientific experiments established that chromosomal abnormalities are indeed causes of certain cancers?

THE PHILADELPHIA CHROMOSOME

In the 1930s and 1940s, scientists examined tumor cells and thought that the number of chromosomes in cancer cells was abnormally high compared to the number of chromosomes in normal cells. Unfortunately, the techniques available at the time were not precise enough

SPOTLIGHT ON CANCER SCIENTISTS
JANET D. ROWLEY (1925–)

Janet Rowley had not planned to be a research scientist. In fact, she did not start doing experiments until she was 36 years old. Nevertheless, Rowley became a first-class scientist who won the prestigious Lasker Award in 1998 for her work demonstrating the relationship between specific chromosomal translocations and particular cancers. One of America's highest honors, the Lasker Awards are often referred to as the American Nobels.

Born in Chicago, Illinois, in 1925, Rowley grew up in a home that encouraged learning. An excellent student, she was awarded a scholarship at the age of 15 to attend a special college program at the University of Chicago, where she completed her last two years of high school and her first two years of college and earned her bachelor's degree. She then stayed at the University of Chicago to complete the requirements for medical school and earned another bachelor's degree. She was only 19 years old at the time. Rowley began her medical studies at the University of Chicago when she was 20. At the time, the number of places available to women who wanted to attend medical school was strictly controlled. Rowley was one of only three women allowed into a class of 65 students.

Rowley married the day after she graduated from medical school. Her husband was also a physician and she decided that she wanted to work part-time while she raised a family. Ultimately, Rowley and her husband had four sons and she worked three days a week for approximately the first 20 years of her career. She began full-time employment when her youngest son was 12 years old.

Rowley's original intention had been to become a clinician. For a while, she worked in a well-baby clinic and then at a clinic for mentally disabled children. She was working with Down syndrome children at that clinic during the late 1950s, when other scientists discovered that Down syndrome is caused by a chromosomal problem. The relationship between a chromosomal defect and a clinical outcome intrigued Rowley.

In 1961, Rowley's husband was going to Oxford to continue his research in pathology. Rowley applied for and received a fellowship to support her own research on chromosomes and perform experiments in **cytogenetics** while overseas. Upon her return to Chicago, Rowley realized that she did

Figure 5.1   Janet Rowley won the 1998 Lasker Award for her work demonstrating the relationship between specific chromosomal translocations and particular cancers. *(Courtesy of the Albert and Mary Lasker Foundation)*

not want to resume her clinical work; she wanted to continue her research. Fortunately, one of her professors from medical school, Dr. Leon Jacobson, had a large amount of grant support and he recognized Rowley's talent. When she approached him for help, he agreed to provide modest support. Rowley could not afford to hire a technician so she gladly did all of the

(continues)

JANET D. ROWLEY

(continued)

experiments herself. Rowley studied the chromosomes of patients who had different types of leukemia. She continued to refine her techniques and, by the early 1970s, was able to show conclusively that chromosomes could exchange pieces or lose pieces and that these chromosomal changes were related to specific cancers. Her work shed light on the relationship between chromosomes and cancer and also helped to provide a roadmap to the specific genes involved in particular cancers. Rowley continues to study chromosome breakage and gene expression in leukemia cells.

to allow an accurate count of the chromosomes in normal cells. This confusion changed in the mid-1950s when methods for culturing and staining cells with dyes and preparing slides for microscopes improved dramatically. It was finally clear that normal human cells contained 46 chromosomes. Accurate comparisons of normal and cancer cells were now possible.

In 1956, American scientist Peter Nowell began to study human leukemia cells. Nowell and his graduate student, David Hungerford, looked at the cells of patients with chronic myelogenous leukemia (CML). Generally speaking, leukemia is a type of cancer in which too many white blood cells are made in the bone marrow, the spongy tissue located in the large bones of the body. CML is one type of leukemia; it accounts for approximately 20 percent of all adult cases. The average age of onset for CML is around 40 to 50 years, and the disease can be fatal in a relatively brief amount of time. People who suffer from CML initially experience fatigue, loss of appetite, a swollen spleen, and anemia, a serious decrease in the number of oxygen-carrying red blood cells in the blood. For many years, no one understood what features in the cells that cause CML were abnormal, and there was no idea how to treat this disease.

In their experiments, Nowell and Hungerford grew cells on microscope slides, stained these cells, and examined the chromosomes to see if there were any changes in number, size, or shape. To their delight, in 1960, Nowell and Hungerford identified an unusual small chromosome in the cancer cells of a CML patient. They examined the chromosomes of many more CML patients and, in each case, this small chromosome was found in cancer cells but never in normal cells. Nowell and Hungerford named the chromosome they found the Philadelphia chromosome in honor of the city in which it was first described. Because methods needed to do experiments to address these questions had not yet been invented, Nowell and Hungerford were not able to learn more about the structure and function of the Philadelphia chromosome and how it produced cancer. Nevertheless, Nowell and Hungerford's findings were the first firm evidence to support Boveri's idea that tumors are the result of chromosomal changes and abnormalities within a single cell.

By the 1970s, techniques for staining chromosomes had improved dramatically and scientists could now compare normal and cancer cells in much more detail. They soon observed that tumor cells were in "disarray." It appeared that chromosomes were broken; some chromosomes were missing pieces while others had extra pieces, and there were extra chromosomes as well as missing chromosomes. One of the most important technical tools was the ability to stain chromosomes so that distinctive stripes or bands were visible. When stained properly, different types of chromosomes exhibit distinctive banding patterns. With staining, it became possible to identify which chromosome was which out of the 23 pairs present in normal human cells.

In 1973, Janet Rowley reexamined CML cells and the Philadelphia chromosome using these new methods. She found that the Philadelphia chromosome was produced by a **reciprocal translocation**, a process in which two chromosomes exchange pieces with each other. In the case of CML, chromosomes 9 and 22 exchange portions. One of the products is a shortened chromosome 22 (the one called the Philadelphia chromosome) and the other is a lengthened chromosome 9. These experiments identified a specific chromosomal abnormality that is associated with a particular cancer. This work was an important breakthrough because it proved that abnormal chromosome function and structure can lead to cancer. The Philadelphia chromosome is not an isolated incident. It is only one example of more than 200 chromosomal abnormalities that are consistently associated with specific types of cancer.

The connection between Rowley's discovery and scientists' understanding of how the breakage and abnormal rejoining of chromosomes can produce cancer had to wait for the development of molecular techniques, such as the ability to visualize tiny segments DNA so that specific genes could be studied. Amazingly, when these studies were undertaken in the late 1970s and early 1980s, the results connected the understanding of chromosomes and cancer with that of oncogenes. In 1984, Dr. Gerard Grosveld and his colleagues showed that reciprocal translocation between chromosomes 9 and 22 moves the *abl* proto-oncogene from chromosome 9 to a site next to the *bcr* gene on chromosome 22. Both the *abl* and *bcr* genes are rendered dysfunctional by this rearrangement and the *abl* is turned into an oncogene. The new fused *bcr-abl* gene gets stuck "on," producing a protein that continually enhances cell division. As a consequence, cell proliferation occurs without control.

Thanks to the discovery of the biochemical abnormality of CML cells, scientists have been able to develop a drug, Gleevec, which blocks activation of the *bcr-abl* protein.

TELOMERES

In the 1930s, Dr. Barbara McClintock, then at the University of Missouri at Columbia, and Dr. H. J. Muller, then at the University of Edinburgh in Scotland, independently reported that there was a special stabilizing structure on the ends of chromosomes. The DNA of these structures, called **telomeres**, was sequenced at Yale University in 1978 by Dr. Elizabeth Blackburn, who showed that there was a simple sequence of nucleotides, the building blocks of DNA, which was repeated multiple times. This DNA did not encode information to make proteins, so what was its function?

Because of the way DNA replication works, it is difficult to replicate entire chromosomes, all the way to their ends. As a result, each time the chromosomes of a cell are replicated in preparation for cell division, they shorten a little bit. As long as the loss is confined to the telomere part of the chromosome, the cell remains healthy. However, each replication shortens the telomeres a little more and, eventually, the telomeres are gone. Because there is no more telomere, functional DNA begins to be lost during replication, and the cell dies. This process gives our cells a finite lifespan—at least under normal circumstances.

Certain cells in the body have a mechanism that prevents the shortening of telomeres. These are the germ cells that will form eggs or sperm. These germ cells bypass the cellular aging mechanism by producing the enzyme **telomerase**, which replaces the telomeres lost at replication. Cancer cells are the only other kinds of cells in the human

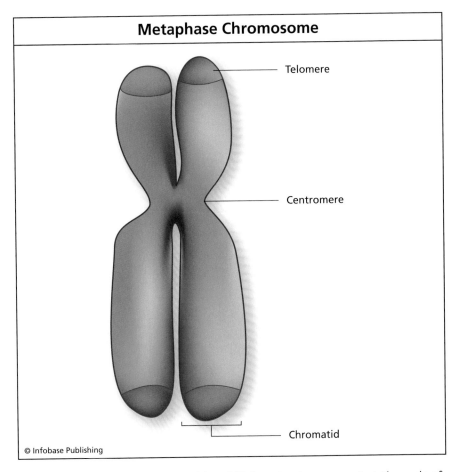

Metaphase Chromosome

Telomere

Centromere

Chromatid

© Infobase Publishing

Figure 5.2 Telomeres are a special stabilizing structure present at the ends of chromosomes. Telomeres protect chromosomes during metaphase, or cell division.

body that can produce telomerase and therefore become immortal. In fact, telomerase is produced by cells in 90 percent of all human tumors. As a consequence, these cells fail to obey the signals that tell them to die even if they are damaged or abnormal. These cells then continue to proliferate and, in all likelihood, accumulate more and more genetic defects that make them even more malignant. The genetic chaos may ultimately become fatal.

SPOTLIGHT ON CANCER SCIENTISTS
ELIZABETH BLACKBURN (1948-)

Affectionately called the "Queen of Telomeres" by other scientists, Elizabeth Blackburn was born in 1948 in Launceston, a small town on the island of Tasmania, off the coast of Australia. She showed an interest in animals and biology from a very early age. In her teens, she decided that she wanted to learn about the underlying mechanisms of biology and devoted herself to studying biochemistry. Blackburn was so excited about the topic that she actually had pictures of amino acids as decorations on the walls of her bedroom.

When Blackburn finished high school, her family moved to the city

Figure 5.3 Elizabeth Blackburn was nicknamed the "Queen of the Telomeres" for her groundbreaking work with this key component of chromosomes. *(AP Photo/Paul Sakuma)*

of Melbourne, Australia. She attended the University of Melbourne and majored in biochemistry. After completing her bachelor's degree, Blackburn moved to England for graduate study. Although the transition from Australia to England was challenging, she thrived at Cambridge University and earned her Ph.D. in 1975. Next came another big move—to the United

(continues)

ELIZABETH BLACKBURN

(continued)

States for a postdoctoral position at Yale. It was there that Blackburn first began her research on telomeres.

Before Blackburn's work, scientists knew that chromosomes had some type of structure on their ends that got shorter with each round of cell division. Thanks to Blackburn and others, researchers now know about the genetic nature of telomeres, including their DNA sequences, and about telomerase, the **enzyme** that is responsible for telomere replication. It is also known that telomerase is not active in most normal human cells, but it is present in 90 percent of human cancer cells.

Today, Blackburn is using the information that she and others have gathered about telomeres and telomerase to develop anticancer therapies that trick cells with active telomerase into making mistakes so that they produce abnormal telomeres, thus triggering cell suicide. Blackburn has said, "Telomeres just grabbed me and kept leading me on. You discover one thing, and then another emerges and you follow that. It keeps unfolding in very unexpected directions."[3]

GENETIC INSTABILITY

One of the ideas that continues to emerge from a consideration of the genetic nature of cancer is that a series of individual events can push a cell in the direction of cancer. There is a tipping point where the mistakes and defects of chromosomes and genes snowball, and the rate of accumulation of problems actually increases. Although it is not true of *all* cancers, an overall genetic instability increases the likelihood that many cancers will develop, with full-blown, malignant invasive tumors.

What produces this genetic instability? Generally, the instability is due to a mutation or a chromosomal defect that generates additional mutations and defects. For example, mutations that interfere with normal DNA replication will produce more mutations. So will mutations that decrease the efficiency or accuracy of DNA repair. A mutation in *RPA1*, a gene known to be necessary for chromosomal repair, results in the production of major chromosome rearrangements, losses, and gains. Mutations that stop apoptosis, or programmed cell death, will also allow mutated and abnormal cells to survive. It is clear that genetic instability aids tremendously in the formation of tumors.

SUMMARY

A full complement of chromosomes is essential for normal cell function. Damaged, rearranged, or lost pieces of chromosomes can lead to many health problems, including cancer. Certain types of cancer are actually associated with specific chromosomal abnormalities. In many cases, the cancer occurs because the chromosomal defect damages a proto-oncogene or tumor suppressor gene. Telomeres—the structures that protect the ends of chromosomes—also play an important role in cancer development. In normal cells, telomere shortening leads to a finite lifespan. In cancer cells, telomeres do not shorten with each division and, as a result, allow cells to become immortal.

6

INHERITED GENES THAT CAN CAUSE CANCER

KEY POINTS

♦ Cancer susceptibility can be inherited.

♦ Approximately 5–10 percent of all human cancers are inherited.

♦ Inheritance of a cancer gene does not mean that the development of the disease is certain, but the probability is higher than for the general population.

♦ Inherited cancers generally involve the malfunction of tumor suppressor genes or problems with genes that are needed for DNA repair.

SPORADIC, FAMILIAL, AND INHERITED CANCERS

All cancers have a genetic basis—mutations in specific genes, oncogenes, and tumor suppressors are critical for a tumor to begin to form.

Cancer is also genetic in that a particular tumor starts with one cell that has accumulated enough mutations to allow it to escape the normal controls of cell proliferation, and, therefore, all of its offspring also inherit these mutations (and will perhaps add some more of their own).

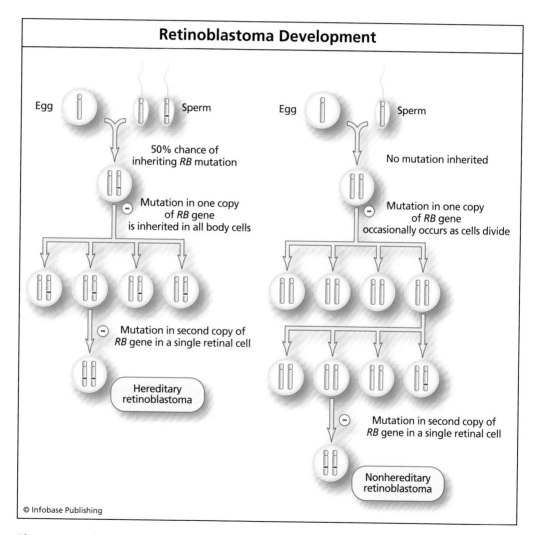

Retinoblastoma Development

Egg   Sperm

50% chance of inheriting *RB* mutation

Mutation in one copy of *RB* gene is inherited in all body cells

Mutation in second copy of *RB* gene in a single retinal cell

Hereditary retinoblastoma

Egg   Sperm

No mutation inherited

Mutation in one copy of *RB* gene occasionally occurs as cells divide

Mutation in second copy of *RB* gene in a single retinal cell

Nonhereditary retinoblastoma

© Infobase Publishing

Figure 6.1   The mutation that leads to retinoblastoma can occur in anyone, but in those who inherit this mutation, the chances of developing retinoblastoma are much greater.

When scientists and physicians analyze the incidence of cancer in people, they recognize three categories of cancers: sporadic, **familial**, and inherited. Sporadic cancers are those for which hereditary factors don't appear to contribute to the cancer risk. There is no family history for the specific cancer and no reason to expect that the genetic element of the disease is anything more than mutations that occurred in a specific cell and ultimately produced a tumor. Sporadic cancers are by far the most common cancers.

Familial cancers are those where there may be some cases of the cancer in a family, but there is no clear pattern. The age of onset is probably not very young and the cancer is found only in one location in the affected individual. In familial cancer, it is unlikely that the cancer will occur in later generations. It is probable that there are hereditary factors and environmental factors that work together to influence the relative risk of developing cancer. Familial cancers are not nearly as common as sporadic ones.

Cancer susceptibility actually can be heritable from parent to child, not just from cell to cell. Inherited cancers are relatively rare, accounting for only 5 to 10 percent of all cancers. Nevertheless, research into these cancers has been important because it has revealed that genes are directly involved in the development of cancer. Moreover, understanding the genes involved in inherited cancers has provided insights into nonhereditary and more common forms of cancer.

Inherited cancers are the least common of all. Here a mutation is inherited in the germline (the sex cells found in the eggs or sperm). As a consequence, every cell in the body has the mutation, not just the tumor cells. If other events go wrong for the cell, the possession of the mutant gene tremendously increases the likelihood that cancer will develop.

THE CASE OF BREAST CANCER

With 180,000 new cases each year in the United States alone, breast cancer is the second most common type of cancer in women. Only skin cancers are more prevalent. Although it is much more common in women, breast cancer occurs in men, too. Breast cancer can be deadly; 45,000 deaths can be attributed to breast cancer each year.

The oldest description of breast tumors dates back to approximately 1600 B.C.E. The Edwin Smith papyrus, discovered in Egypt, describes eight cases of breast cancer. The Egyptian record explains that the cancers were cauterized, or burned, with a tool called a fire drill. According to the papyrus, the doctors of ancient Egypt recognized that there was little they could do to treat breast cancer successfully.

Concern about breast cancer in the ancient world was not limited to Egypt. Artifacts found in the remains of ancient Greek temples include clay statues of female bodies with breast tumors. Some people speculate that these statues were used in prayer by individuals seeking supernatural help. The famous Greek healer Hippocrates thought that the disease was a by-product of a melancholic, or sad, disposition. Galen, the eminent physician of ancient Rome, agreed.

Observations and ideas regarding what causes breast cancer have been wide-ranging and quite creative throughout medical history. Dr. Domenico Antonio Rigoni-Stern examined mortality statistics collected between 1760 and 1839 in Verona, Italy. He noted that of 994 women who died during that time period, more than 30 percent died of breast cancer. Interestingly, nuns were more likely to die of breast cancer than were married women. This observation suggested that something about not bearing children increased the likelihood of breast cancer. In the 1880s, the English physician Dr. John Snow attributed breast cancer to the "debilitated" lifestyles and "neuroses" of "civilized" women. In other words, Snow thought that women were simply nervous and not leading healthy lifestyles and consequently were developing breast tumors. He mentioned a cause of cancer was "the universal habit amongst civilized women in Europe and the U.S.A. of wearing bodily constricting corsets from a young age."[4] In the opinion of the medical professionals of Snow's day, breast cancer appeared to be due to problems with a woman's mental and emotional outlook, exacerbated by the chronic irritation produced by tight undergarments! Physicians also thought that breast cancer was the result of grief. Here are two cases that "explain" the onset of breast cancer, the first by Richard Guy in 1759 and the second by Herbert Snow (no relation to John) in 1883:

> *Case 1:* The Wife of a Mate of a Ship (who was taken some Time ago by the French, and put in Prison) was thereby so much affected, that her breast began to swell, and soon after broke out in a desperate cancer which had proceeded so far that I could not undertake her case. She never before had any complaint in her breast.[5]

> *Case 2:* Emma B., aged 49; single. No family history; no blow or injury. School mistress. Has had more or less trouble for years; had a carbuncle [a painful inflammation] on the shoulder three years ago; and has not felt strong since. Has been much over-worked at school. Says that last June she felt almost out of her mind, and was ready to throw herself out of the window. Father was ill in bed for six months last year; had much anxiety about him, and for several months at the beginning of 1883 pecuniary [money-related] troubles. The tumours appeared about Christmas last.[6]

It is important to note that extensive research done in the 1960s, 1970s, and 1980s revealed no associations or relationships between the onset of breast cancer and prior stressful life events. Moreover, there is no relationship between a woman's (or man's) personality and the likelihood of developing breast cancer. The next section will consider what is known about what actually causes breast cancer.

A FAMILY LINK

One of the early observations that did lead to an increased understanding of cancer was made by the ancient Greeks, who described families that were "plagued" by breast cancer. Writings from the Romans dating back to 100 C.E. also reported the clustering of breast cancers in certain families but not in others. In the 1860s, the eminent French neurosurgeon and anthropologist Paul Broca analyzed the incidence of breast cancer in his wife's family. He examined medical records for four generations of the family and noted 10 cases of breast cancer occurring in 24 individuals. By doing a **pedigree** analysis, Broca demonstrated quite clearly that there was an inherited disposition for developing breast cancer.

In 1926, the British government's Ministry of Health documented evidence that the first-degree relatives (children, siblings, or parents) of women with breast cancer had a greater risk of developing breast cancer than did individuals without such a relative. Beginning in the 1970s, and continuing through the present, scientists have done studies to learn more about the possible inheritance of an increased risk for breast cancer. The link proving a person's chances of developing breast cancer and the incidence of cancer in family members has been strengthened. It is known that the first-degree relatives of individuals with breast cancer have a significantly higher risk of developing breast cancer themselves. Moreover, the risk is even greater if the onset of cancer is early (when the patient is under age 50) or bilateral (in both breasts). An individual's risk also increases as the number of relatives with breast cancer increases. Susceptibility to breast cancer can be inherited from either the mother's *or* the father's side of the family. All of these observations and connections point to the idea that there are inherited genes that increase the risk of developing breast cancer.

BREAST CANCER GENES

Approximately 10 percent of all breast cancers are due to the inheritance of cancer-causing genes from one's mother or father. A search for the identity of these genes was initiated in 1974 by Dr. Mary-Claire King, a geneticist now working at the University of Washington. In 1990, King succeeded in mapping *BRCA1*, a gene that, when mutated, significantly increases the risk of breast and ovarian cancers. In 1994, a research group in Utah cloned *BRCA1,* and another breast cancer-causing gene, *BRCA2*, was discovered. More than 300 different *BRCA1* and 100 *BRCA2* mutations have been described so far. While the lifetime risk of breast cancer for women in the general population is around 12 percent, people who have inherited mutant *BRCA1* and *BRCA2* genes have an 80 percent chance of developing breast cancer by the age of 70. Although inherited breast cancer accounts for only 10 percent of all breast cancers, mutations in *BRCA1* and *BRCA2* are responsible for 80 percent of these inherited cases. Evidently there is something quite important about the normal functioning of *BRCA1* and *BRCA2*. What are the functions of the proteins that are encoded by these genes?

   BRCA1 encode for a large protein that normally functions in the nucleus of the cell, the site where chromosomes are located. Many of the hundreds of mutations that have been described for *BRCA1* result in the production of a shortened, dysfunctional protein. Experiments have shown that the normal *BRCA1* protein, in conjunction with other proteins, serves many important functions in the cell, including tumor suppression and DNA repair. *BRCA2* also encodes for a protein needed for tumor suppression and DNA repair. Properly functioning tumor suppressor genes are essential for avoiding cancer, and a cell that cannot repair DNA errors or damage is much more likely to become cancerous.

Even though the inheritance of mutations in *BRCA1* and *BRCA2* genes increases a person's chance of developing breast cancer very dramatically, it is important to note that the risk is not 100 percent. Not everyone who has the mutations for these genes will develop breast cancer. In spite of their important role in breast cancer susceptibility, *BRCA1* and *BRCA2* mutant genes are not the only factors involved. Other genes and even the environment can impact the effects of the mutant *BRCA1* and *BRCA2*.

OTHER INHERITED CANCERS

In addition to breast cancer, several other types of cancer have inherited forms. Approximately 5 to 10 percent of all colon, ovary, prostate, and thyroid cancer, as well as melanoma, are inherited. *BRCA1* and *BRCA2* mutations are directly involved in inherited ovarian cancer and, as we will see in Chapter 7, the gene *APC* encodes for a tumor suppressor associated with colon cancer.

Many cancers that occur in childhood or early adulthood are due to an inheritance of increased susceptibility. For example, retinoblastoma, a cancer of the retina, can occur even before birth. In the inherited form of the disease, the gene *RB* is mutated or missing. Wilms' tumor, a type of kidney malignancy, is due to the inheritance of a mutant *WT-1* gene. *RB* and *WT-1* both encode for tumor suppressors. As we saw in Chapter 1, xeroderma pigmentosum, a disease that results in skin cancer at a very

SPOTLIGHT ON CANCER SCIENTISTS
ALFRED KNUDSON (1922–)

When Alfred Knudson started college at the California Institute of Technology (Caltech), he knew that he liked science and numbers. At Caltech, Knudson discovered biology, and he began a lifelong interest in genetics, a field that utilized his interests in both science and numbers.

While there, Knudson enlisted in to the Naval Reserve V-12 program, under whose auspices he attended Columbia University's College of Physicians and Surgeons. Later, as a pediatric intern at New York Hospital, he encountered children with cancer across the street at Memorial-Sloan Kettering Hospital and was introduced to the research problem that he has continued to study his entire life: pediatric cancers, especially those that were found in young children—the so-called "embryonal tumors."

Figure 6.2 Alfred Knudson's research laid the foundation for contemporary efforts to understand both hereditary cancers and tumor suppressors. *(Courtesy of the Albert and Mary Lasker Foundation)*

young age, is due to the inheritance of a faulty version of a gene necessary for DNA repair. Li-Fraumeni syndrome, which was described in Chapter 4, involves the inheritance of a mutant *p53* gene. Consequently, the tumor suppressor *p53* is rendered nonfunctional.

Knudson returned to Caltech in 1953 to earn his Ph.D. and to learn how to study cancer both scientifically and clinically. After studying childhood leukemia for a while, Knudson turned his attention to solid tumors found in children, particularly retinoblastoma. In studies done in the late 1960s and reported in the early 1970s, Knudson observed that retinoblastoma occurred in both **hereditary** and nonhereditary forms. In hereditary cases, children developed tumors in both eyes or in multiple sites in one eye, and the onset of the disease occurred at a very early age, often in infants. In contrast, the onset is later in nonhereditary retinoblastoma, in which a single tumor forms in one eye.

From this information, Knudson hypothesized that children with hereditary retinoblastoma inherited a mutant gene that predisposed them to cancer and that another mutation was necessary for the disease to develop. In nonhereditary retinoblastoma, two mutations had to occur for a tumor to appear. Knudson developed a mathematical model of the two-hit hypothesis that incorporated clinical data. He also proposed that the defect was in a tumor suppressor gene and he studied the chromosomes of retinoblastoma cells and located where the gene is positioned. Ultimately, the gene in question, *RB1*, was cloned by another laboratory. Knudson's work laid the foundation for the research being done today on both hereditary cancers and tumor suppressors.

Are any features common to inherited cancer-causing genes? The answer is yes. Most (and maybe all) inherited cancers involve genes that are essential for tumor suppression, DNA repair, or both. However, these inherited genes don't operate alone. The next chapter looks in detail at a cancer with an inherited cancer-causing gene *and* the other genes involved in the process of tumor formation.

SUMMARY

Although most cancers are not passed from parent to offspring, approximately 5 to 10 percent of cancers are due to an inherited susceptibility to the disease. In such inherited cancers, the likelihood of developing one or more tumors can be quite high. In most cases, inherited cancer susceptibility involves defective tumor suppressor genes or problems with genes needed for accurate DNA repair. Research into inherited cancers has revealed a great deal of important information about nonhereditary forms as well.

7

How Many Genetic Mistakes Are Needed to Produce Cancer?

KEY POINTS

- The likelihood of developing cancer increases with age.

- A comparison of inherited and non-inherited cancers reveals that the development of cancer is a multi-step process.

- This multistep process involves initiation, promotion, and progression.

- Several genetic changes are required for the development of a malignancy.

- Studies of colon cancer have revealed an association between the accumulation of specific gene defects and the progressive development of a tumor.

CHARACTERISTICS OF CANCER CELLS

There is a relatively small set of characteristics shared by cancer cells

♦ uncontrolled cell proliferation

♦ poor communication between cells

♦ lack of cell differentiation

♦ failure to commit cell suicide when it is appropriate to do so

♦ faulty cell adhesion

♦ ability to invade other tissues

♦ immortalization

Cancer can be caused by mutations in tumor suppressor genes or proto-oncogenes, or chromosomal problems that affect the structure or function of tumor suppressor genes or proto-oncogenes. These genetic defects can result in tumor formation whether the flaws are brand-new or inherited from parents. The question remains: How do these genetic mistakes work together to cause cancer? Is a defect in any one of the genes enough, or do several genes need to go bad? Does cancer happen all at once, or is it the outcome of a multistep process?

THE MULTISTEP PROCESS OF CARCINOGENESIS

Experiments with, and studies of, the patterns of human cancers make it clear that cancer results from the accumulation of many genetic defects. **Tumorigenesis** is indeed a multistep process. First, cancer is generally a disease of old age. Although there are some cancers that affect children and young adults, the vast majority of tumors appear in people older

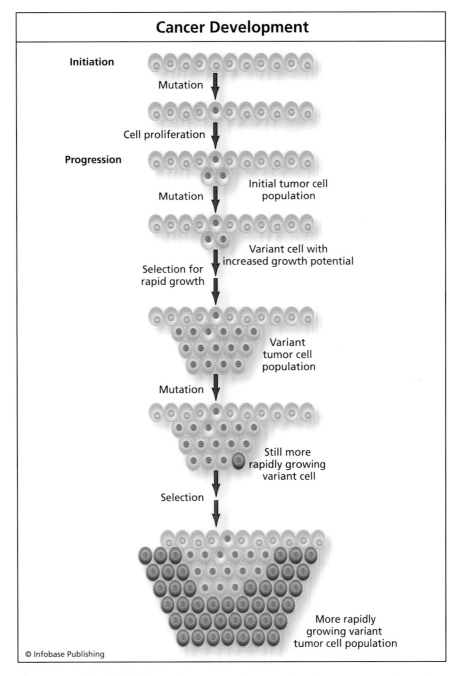

Figure 7.1 The initiation and progress of cancer involves numerous steps of cell growth and mutation.

than 50. In fact, cancer incidence increases in direct proportion to age. If only one mutation were needed for cancer to form, then the incidence of the disease would be unrelated to age. Mathematical analyses of the patterns of cancers in human populations calculate that somewhere between four and six genetic changes are needed for a full-blown malignancy to develop.

A second line of evidence indicating that cancer formation is a multi-step process comes from inherited cancers. In the case of retinoblastoma, a cancer of the retina, inheritance of a faulty *RB* tumor suppressor gene often results in the early onset of the disease—sometimes in infancy—as well as the development of tumors in both eyes. In contrast, sporadic or nonhereditary retinoblastoma rarely produces tumors in both eyes and the age of onset is older. The explanation for the difference between the inherited and sporadic forms of retinoblastoma was articulated in Alfred Knudson's "two-hit" hypothesis. Knudson postulated that more than one hit, or mutation, was needed for retinoblastoma or other cancers to form. In those people with inherited retinoblastoma, one hit had already occurred before birth; they had inherited a mutated *RB* tumor suppressor gene. Only one more hit was needed for the disease to appear. Hence, it did so when patients were very young. In those patients with nonhereditary retinoblastoma, two hits were needed to knock out the tumor suppressor function. This takes more time, and consequently, the onset of the disease came later.

EXPERIMENTAL EVIDENCE FOR A MULTISTEP MECHANISM

The multistep nature of carcinogenesis was first revealed in experiments done long before anyone knew anything about cancer genes. In the early 1960s, scientists discovered that mice developed tumors after being fed dimethylbenz[a]anthracene (DMBA), a carcinogen found in tobacco smoke, followed by skin exposure to croton oil, a component of the seeds of a specific type of shrub that causes skin inflammation. Interestingly, the ingestion of DMBA by itself did not cause cancer, nor did exposure to croton oil alone. However, DMBA ingestion followed by croton oil exposure did produce cancer, even if animals were fed DMBA just once with an entire year elapsing before their exposure to croton oil. Amazingly, if croton oil exposure occurred before the ingestion of DMBA, no tumors formed.

These results showed that more than one step was necessary for cancer to develop. The first step, **initiation**, is the conversion of cells to a precancerous state. DMBA accomplished this. The second step, **promotion**, is the stimulation of cell division in the altered cells so that a tumor grows. Croton oil was responsible for this step.

Generally speaking, tumor initiators work by damaging DNA. A single exposure can be sufficient to cause this damage. Tumor promoters work more gradually and require repeated or lengthy exposure. Promoting agents stimulate cell division. Initiation produces mutated cells and promotion increases the number of mutated cells in the affected tissue or organ. The next step, tumor **progression**, occurs when cells change their characteristics as they continue to divide, evade the body's defenses, and survive. Ultimately, these cells become very dangerous to the body.

Once scientists learned about oncogenes and tumor suppressor genes, they did experiments to discover the minimal genetic changes needed for cancer development. In one experiment, **fibroblasts**—a type of cell that produces connective or support tissues in the body—were grown in culture dishes and had two types of oncogenes added to them either one at a time or together. When the oncogenes *c-myc* or *rasD* were added separately, the fibroblasts did not transform; they remained normal. In contrast, fibroblast cells that took in both *c-myc* and *rasD* genes underwent transformation and became cancerous. Evidently, it took at least two oncogenes to do the job; one was insufficient. In a similar experiment done in mice, the *c-myc* gene was able to cause mammary tumors in a small number of mice in 100 days, while *rasD* alone did so in 50 percent of mice in 150 days. However, when *c-myc* and *rasD* were present together, mammary tumors appeared much more quickly than with either oncogene alone.

EVIDENCE FOR MULTISTEP CARCINOGENESIS IN HUMANS

Experimental evidence from animal studies provides substantial support for the theory that cells need to accumulate several mutations before tumors will form. Do direct observations of human cancers fit in this theory, too? The answer to this question is an unequivocal yes.

An examination of the specific genetic alterations in various tumors reveals that cells within a particular tumor all contain some common genetic changes. Yet the changes observed in one tumor will often be different from those observed in another tumor. These observations make sense, because each individual tumor starts with one mutated cell that gives it a slight advantage in growth. If one of the daughter cells of this original cell undergoes a mutation, even more growth would be enhanced. A third mutation in a cell of this tumor would produce a cell that would outgrow all the others, and all of the offspring of this cell would have the same three mutations. This process could continue until enough mutations accumulate to allow a metastatic cancer to develop.

MORE EVIDENCE: COLON CANCER

In 1494, Ferrante I of Aragon, the king of Naples, died at the age of 63. As was appropriate for a man of his place in society during his time,

Ferrante I was embalmed and placed in a wooden sarcophagus in the Abbey of San Domenico Maggiore in Naples. In the late 1990s, Ferrante's body was exhumed and examined externally and internally by surgery. Scientists found a well-preserved tumor in the body's pelvic region. A team of scientists from the Institute of Pathology at Pisa University cut the tumor into thin sections for microscopic examination. They determined that the tumor was probably an **adenocarcinoma** from the large intestine. Evidently, Ferrante I had suffered from colon cancer. The tumor was preserved well enough for scientists to collect DNA from it. Analysis of the DNA revealed that the oncogene *ras* was mutated. As discussed below, *ras* is one of a sequence of genes that becomes mutated in the multistep pathway that leads to the development of colon cancer.

Cancer of the colon and/or rectum (often called colorectal cancer) is one of the most common malignancies in the United States and Western Europe. It is also one of the leading causes of cancer deaths worldwide. In the United States alone, approximately 140,000 new cases are diagnosed each year, and at least 50,000 people will die each year as well from the disease. Interestingly, the incidence of colorectal cancer is as much as 20 times higher in populations in developed nations, compared to the populations in developing nations. In fact, by the age of 70, about 50 percent of individuals in Western countries will have an **adenoma**, a benign tumor that, if left untreated, will likely become malignant.

The study of one form of colon cancer, **familial adenomatous polyposis (FAP)**, has been particularly helpful in determining the progression of mutations that lead to invasive, malignant cancer. FAP is associated with an inherited mutation in the tumor suppressor gene *APC*. People with FAP grow thousands of **polyps**, or benign growths, in their colons. If this condition is left untreated, there is an almost 100 percent risk that the individual will develop colon cancer by the age of 60. Although

SPOTLIGHT ON CANCER SCIENTISTS
BERT VOGELSTEIN (1949-)

When Bert Vogelstein was a child, he did not enjoy school much even though he liked to learn. His solution to this dilemma was to skip school a few days every week and go to the public library to read. He did this for years until he had read just about everything in his small local library. It was not until college that Vogelstein started to pay attention in school. He became intrigued by math and even started graduate study to get his Ph.D. Vogelstein then decided to go to medical school and become a physician.

While in medical school at Johns Hopkins University in Baltimore, Vogelstein's hometown, he got experience doing research. For a while, he was not sure whether to practice medicine or become a full-time researcher. An experience he had as a medical intern helped him make up

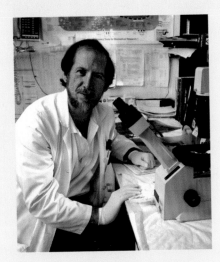

Figure 7.2 Cancer researcher Bert Vogelstein also plays keyboards in a band called Wild Type, which donates all proceeds from its performances to cancer research. *(Alen McWeeny/Corbis)*

FAP accounts for less than 1 percent of all colon cancers, *APC* mutations are found in approximately two-thirds of nonhereditary colon cancers. Consequently, an understanding of *APC* and other gene mutations that are involved in FAP can be applied to colon cancer in general.

his mind. A four-year-old girl was brought into the hospital by her parents. Vogelstein examined her, ran tests, and diagnosed the problem as cancer. He saw the terrible looks on the parents' faces and was struck by the fact that he could not explain to them why their daughter had developed cancer. What could cause cancer in a four-year-old? He decided that the answer could ultimately only be found through research.

At first, Vogelstein tried to see patients during the day and do research in the evening, but then he realized that the research made him happier and that he would have a better chance of making a contribution by working hard on just one thing.

Vogelstein has made several contributions to our understanding of cancer. Especially noteworthy are the studies where Vogelstein and his colleagues found genes that cause colon cancer and established a genetic model for cancer progression. Vogelstein's research has always considered the practical applications that can benefit patients. Today, he is working on methods to detect cancer early, when treatment is more feasible. He is also developing techniques to target cancer cells and tumors for destruction without harming normal healthy cells and tissues.

Vogelstein is the keyboardist in a musical band called Wild Type, along with other cancer researchers. They play at science conferences and at local Baltimore bars. Any money they make is donated to cancer charities.

Dr. Bert Vogelstein, along with other scientists, examined the sequential stages in the development of colon cancer in people with FAP, starting with small benign polyps, to larger benign adenomas, all the way to invasive carcinomas. Vogelstein not only looked at the structure

of the tissues at each stage, but he also characterized the genetic alterations that were present at each step. In fact, Vogelstein was able to align
the accumulation of genetic mutations with particular stages of tumor
development. Amazingly, these genetic errors occurred in a general, if
somewhat variable, sequence.

First, the loss of a functional *APC* gene results in polyp formation.
As mentioned earlier, *APC* is a tumor suppressor gene that normally
codes for a protein that stops the cell growth and division cycle.
When normal APC protein is missing, the protein myc is produced
inappropriately. Since the *myc* gene encodes for a protein that triggers
cell division, extra cell proliferation occurs. The next mutation often
occurs in *ras*, a proto-oncogene that encodes for a molecule important
in cell communication. Because of this mutation, even more cell division is triggered, and a benign adenoma develops. The next genetic
alteration involves the loss of *DCC*, a gene that encodes a protein that
is important in cell adhesion. As a result, the adenoma grows even
larger. Finally, a mutation that inactivates the tumor suppressor *p53*
results in a malignant carcinoma.

The DNA isolated from human colon carcinomas usually contains all
four of these mutations. Although the sequence of these genetic events
is not always exactly the same and some other genes may play roles, it
is clear that various mutations involving both oncogenes and tumor suppressor genes lead to colon cancer. Because tumorigenesis requires an
accumulation of mutations, it can take decades for cancer to develop.

SUMMARY

The chance of growing a tumor increases as a person gets older. The
reason for this relationship between cancer and age is that several

genetic changes are needed for a malignancy to develop, and these can take time to occur. The multistep progression of tumor development has been especially well-studied in colon cancer. Here, scientists have established a clear association between the sequential mutations of a series of specific tumor suppressor genes and oncogenes, and the gradual development of an invasive malignancy.

8

FUTURE HOPES, CHALLENGES, AND QUESTIONS

KEY POINTS

♦ There are sensitive techniques available for the early diagnosis of many types of cancer.

♦ There are medical tests that can determine whether people possess inherited cancer susceptibility genes.

♦ It is now known that in addition to mutation, epigenetic changes of gene function are important in cancer development.

♦ Microarray analysis allows scientists to compare the activity of thousands of genes in normal cells and cancer cells. This type of test can be used to diagnose cancer and characterize tumors for treatment.

♦ The protein products of cancer genes can be monitored for diagnosis.

♦ Knowledge about cancer genes has resulted in the development of new cancer treatments.

A DIAGNOSIS OF THE PAST

In 1967, the U.S. Vice President Hubert Humphrey noticed blood in his urine and went to see his doctor to find out what was wrong. The physician examined Humphrey and collected a urine sample. Examination of the sample did not reveal any abnormal cells, so doctors did not diagnose bladder cancer. Consequently, aggressive treatment was not initiated. The doctors' actions made a lot of sense at the time because, after all, there are several reasons why blood might be found in urine, none of which have anything to do with cancer. Unfortunately, the initial diagnosis was incorrect and only a few years later, after more symptoms had become evident, Humphrey was diagnosed with bladder cancer. In 1976, Humphrey had extensive surgery and underwent radiation therapy. Sadly, the disease recurred, and he died in 1978.

The late 1970s and early 1980s marked the birth of many molecular biological techniques that are now routinely used in research labs. In 1994, scientists from Johns Hopkins University obtained permission from Muriel Humphrey, Hubert Humphrey's widow, to examine the medical samples that had been collected from her husband 27 years earlier. She agreed, saying,

> This is what Hubert would have wanted; this is what kept him going, I believe, and this is why we wanted his records to be preserved for future use. Hubert and I had a philosophy that saw us through many hard times. It was "Everything happens for the best." Often, it takes a long time to know why. Through many years of grief and anger, I couldn't relate our philosophy to his suffering and death. Perhaps now I have the answer.[7]

The scientists analyzed both the urine samples that had been stored frozen since 1967 and tumor samples that had been preserved for decades. The researchers knew that mutations in the *p53* tumor suppressor gene are found in bladder cancer. They wondered whether they could detect this mutant gene in urine samples from 1967.

When they tested the tumor itself, they found clear evidence of the *p53* mutation. Amazingly, this same mutation was also identified in the cells present in the urine sample taken so much earlier. If the technique used in this experiment had been available in 1967, the mutated *p53* gene could have been identified and a diagnosis of bladder cancer could have been made years before it was. It is likely that an earlier diagnosis and immediate surgery might have saved Humphrey's life.

PRACTICAL BENEFITS AND APPLICATIONS FROM UNDERSTANDING CANCER GENETICS

Our present knowledge of cancer genes enables doctors to make an earlier diagnosis, giving cancer patients the promise of improved treatment success. Genetic testing of individuals for their cancer risk, characterization of tumors for treatment planning, accurate predictions of disease outcomes, and even the development of new cancer treatments are all areas where a great deal of progress has occurred, thanks to our understanding of cancer genes and how they work.

Testing

Inherited cancers account for 5 to 10 percent of all malignancies. For many of these cancers, people can be tested to see if they have specific mutant genes. For example, tests are available for the *BRCA1* and *BRCA2* mutations that are associated with hereditary breast and ovarian cancers. Similarly, tests currently exist to screen for the inherited cancer genes involved in retinoblastoma, Li-Fraumeni syndrome, and familial adenomatous polyposis (FAP), among others.

Tests for the presence of inherited cancer genes are generally done only for people in high-risk groups—for example, a family that has a pattern of cancer that is consistent with inherited cancer susceptibility such as retinoblastoma or breast cancer. The goal of the tests is to let people know their relative cancer risk. Should the test results be positive, it would simply mean that the individual's risk for cancer may be very high, although cancer is by no means a certainty. For such people, more frequent medical examinations to allow for earlier detection and treatment, efforts to prevent certain cancers by using hormone therapy or changing their diet, or even preventive surgery may be options. For individuals with a negative test result, the risk of cancer is the same as that for other people in the population.

In many cases, people from high-risk families decide not to be tested for inherited cancer genes. They may have several reasons, including concerns about privacy and whether potential employers or health insurers could gain access to the information and discriminate against them.

Diagnosis

The sensitive molecular techniques that have been developed over the past few years have made it possible to diagnose cancer much more easily from very small cell or tissue samples. In fact, it is possible to analyze blood, urine, or other bodily fluids and identify certain types of tumors when they are quite small and not detectable by other means. For example, scientists have examined stool samples to see whether they could detect mutant genes in the cells normally sloughed off the lining of the colon when solid wastes move through the digestive system. One of the most common mutated genes in colon cancer is *ras*. If such mutations could be detected in colon cells present in stool samples, diagnosis of developing colon cancer could be made even earlier than

SPOTLIGHT ON CANCER SCIENTISTS
GEORGE H. HITCHINGS (1905–1998)

When George Hitchings was 12 years old, his father died after a prolonged illness. This loss made a deep impression on Hitchings and made him turn his attention toward pursuing a career in medicine. As the student speaker at his high school graduation, Hitchings delivered an address about French scientist Louis Pasteur. To Hitchings, Pasteur's ability to combine basic research with practical outcomes was not only admirable but would become the model Hitchings emulated throughout his career.

While at the University of Washington, Hitchings found himself enchanted by chemistry. He earned both his bachelor's and master's degrees in that subject. Next, he earned a Ph.D. in chemistry from Harvard University. Unfortunately for Hitchings, the next nine years were a challenge. Starting in 1933, during the Great Depression, work was hard to find, even with a Ph.D. from Harvard. Hitchings took a series of temporary appointments and worked on various research projects. Finally, in 1942, he was hired by the Wellcome Research Laboratories. Hitchings was appointed the head and only member of the biochemistry department. At long last, he was able to develop his own research program. Over time, the research group grew. Hitchings spent the rest of his career at the pharmaceutical company that eventually became Burroughs-Wellcome (and is now part of GlaxoSmithKline).

Hitchings' research program focused on rational drug design. He and the scientists in his group designed new molecules with specific molecular structures. Their designs were based on what was known about the structure and function of molecules that occur inside cells. For example,

Hitchings and his colleague Gertrude Elion synthesized compounds that resembled the natural components of DNA, purines, and pyrimidines. These compounds interfered with DNA replication and, therefore, the division of cancer cells. Hitchings and Elion received the Nobel Prize for Physiology or Medicine in 1988 for their research. Hitchings' team developed successful treatments for a variety of diseases, including malaria, gout, and viral infection. They also designed drugs to prevent the rejection of transplanted organs. In 1967, Hitchings became vice president in charge

Figure 8.1   Losing his father to a prolonged illness at age 12 inspired George Hitchings to pursue a career in medicine. *(AP)*

of research at Burroughs-Wellcome, a position he held until he retired in 1976. After he officially retired, he resumed his research and also helped support the work of other scientists by running a philanthropic organization called the Burroughs-Wellcome Fund. When he was awarded the Nobel Prize, Hitchings recalled that "when I was baptized, my father held me up and dedicated my life to the service of mankind. I am very proud that, in some small measure, I have been able to fulfill his hopes."[8]

was possible with the visual observation of polyps. When stool samples are analyzed for the presence of mutated *ras* oncogenes, the mutations are indeed found in some people.

In addition to examining cells and tissues for the presence of individual oncogenes or mutated tumor suppressors, it is possible to do a global analysis of gene activity in cancer cells. The technique called **microarray** analysis allows scientists to monitor the activity of tens of thousands of genes at the same time rather than looking at just one gene at a time. This method can be used to compare cancer cells and normal cells to establish detailed genetic activity profiles of each cell that could be helpful for diagnosis.

Another strategy for detecting cancer is to look for the protein products of cancer genes. The common screen for prostate cancer relies upon detection of PSA, a protein that becomes elevated in individuals with prostate cancer but is not present at high levels in people who don't have the disease. The detection of telomerase, the enzyme that rejuvenates the ends of a chromosome, also indicates the presence of cancer cells, since this molecule is not present in most normal human cells. Whether the tests involve looking at individual genes, the activity of many genes, or the protein products of gene activity, anything that aids in making an earlier diagnosis of cancer increases the likelihood of successful treatment, since most cancers become more and more difficult to control as they progress and tumors become more malignant and invasive.

CHARACTERIZING TUMORS AND PERSONALIZING TREATMENT

Techniques used for diagnosis and screening of individuals are also effective for evaluating the seriousness of a particular tumor. By characterizing the specific mutations that are present in tumor cells, it is sometimes possible to tailor treatment for individual tumors and to make accurate predictions about the prognosis, or outcome, of the disease. For example, amplification of *erbB-2* genes in breast and ovarian cancers predicts that the disease is likely to progress rapidly. Amplification is the replication of many copies of a gene and their insertions back into the chromosome. When a gene is amplified, the protein it codes is overproduced. Similarly, amplification of *N-myc* genes in neuroblastoma also indicates a very serious form of the disease. In both cases, detecting these specific genes in the tumor cells of patients would encourage a more aggressive form of treatment for cancer.

In the case of childhood acute leukemia, genetic analysis of the cancers of newly diagnosed patients may be able to improve the already impressive cure rate of more than 70 percent. Research has shown that patients who display certain favorable genetic features in their cancer respond best to a conventional drug therapy that minimizes long-term side effects. In contrast, patients whose genetic profiles reveal high-risk features, such as a *bcr-abl* gene fusion, described in Chapter 5, are candidates for more aggressive treatments, such as bone marrow transplantation.

As is the case for diagnosis, microarray analysis is helpful in characterizing cancers so that treatments can be optimized. For example, large B-cell lymphoma appears to come in two types. Microarray analysis has revealed that each type of lymphoma shows a distinct gene activity profile. As a result, it is possible to evaluate individual cases of the disease, determine appropriate treatments, and make reliable prognoses about the likely outcomes for specific patients.

Treatment

Knowledge of cancer gene structure and function has enabled scientists to develop cancer treatments that target specific genes or their protein products. This area of research holds a great deal of promise for the future. Already, there are two exciting examples of successes in this effort.

The first, Gleevec, is a drug used to treat chronic myelogenous leukemia (CML). As discussed in Chapter 5, CML is a type of cancer that occurs in people who have the so-called Philadelphia chromosome. The chromosomal translocation that produces the Philadelphia chromosome results in the juxtaposition of two genes, *bcr* and the oncogene *abl*. The fused *bcr-abl* gene produces an abnormal version of a molecule that triggers cell proliferation. This abnormal molecule will not respond to the cell's normal stop signals and, as a consequence, cell division continues. Gleevec interferes with the functioning of the abnormal protein and prevents it from activating cell proliferation. In this way, the cancer is controlled.

The second example is Herceptin, a drug that is an effective treatment of certain types of breast cancer. In approximately 30 percent of breast cancers, the *erbB-2* protein is present in too large an amount because of the amplification of the gene that encodes it. The *erbB-2* is a receptor molecule found in the cell membrane of breast cells. When activated, it tells cells to divide. When too much *erbB-2* is present, cell proliferation is unregulated. Herceptin binds to *erbB-2* and stops it from encouraging cell division. As a result, control over cell proliferation is regained.

In both of these examples, the successful drug was designed to target the protein products of abnormal cancer-causing genes. Research is now underway to add more drugs to the arsenal available to fight cancer. Examples of treatments being developed include some to stop the function of the protein products of the *ras* oncogenes, others to restore the activity of an abnormal *p53* tumor suppressor so that cancer cells will obey "orders" to commit suicide, and even some that target abnormal

RB tumor suppressor proteins, which is the molecule associated with retinoblastoma and some other cancers, too.

FUTURE RESEARCH AND QUESTIONS

The great gains in our basic understanding of cancer genes have allowed scientists to develop techniques to test whether high-risk individuals have inherited cancer-causing genes; to diagnose cancer much earlier than ever before, increasing the chances of successful treatment; to characterize tumors so that treatments can be more individualized and predictions about outcomes will be more accurate; and to develop therapies that target specific cancer genes and their protein products. There have been many exciting successes so far, and research continues in these promising areas. It seems likely that the best is yet to come as we keep learning about cancer genes and the regulatory pathways that control cell behaviors. In addition to the research being done to improve detection, diagnosis, and treatment, there are other important areas of inquiry that still remain open to scientists and physicians.

Epigenetic Control of Genes

Although it is true that mutations in the DNA of tumor suppressor genes or in proto-oncogenes can lead to an accumulation of genetic errors that may result in cancer, scientists have discovered other mechanisms whereby faulty genes can lead to tumor formation. For example, in some cases, changes in the concentrations of proteins that regulate tumor suppressor gene or proto-oncogene function can disrupt the normal behaviors of these genes, even though they have not actually mutated. Reversible chemical changes can also occur in DNA, making gene expression operate incorrectly. This type of alteration is

SPOTLIGHT ON CANCER SCIENTISTS
GERTRUDE B. ELION (1918–1999)

Although she was initially hired as George Hitchings' lab assistant, Gertrude Elion very quickly exhibited her remarkable talent and drive as a research scientist in her own right. She and Hitchings shared the 1988 Nobel Prize for Physiology or Medicine for the development of drugs for cancer and other diseases.

Elion was born in 1918 in New York City, the child of immigrants from Eastern Europe. She was an excellent student who was unsure what she would study when she went to college. The death of her beloved grandfather from stomach cancer when Elion was 15 helped her to decide. She became motivated to do something that could lead to a cure for this terrible disease.

When it came time for Elion to go to college, finances were very difficult for the family. Like many other Americans, Elion's father lost everything in the stock market crash of 1929. Fortunately, there were some free colleges in New York City for students with excellent academic records. Elion was admitted to Hunter College, where she majored in chemistry.

Upon graduation, Elion tried to go to graduate school but there were

Figure 8.2 Gertrude Elion began work as George Hitching's lab assistant before going on to become a successful research scientist. *(AP)*

not many openings or much financial support, especially for women. She took an unpaid job as a lab assistant for a chemist because she thought the experience would be worthwhile. After a year and a half of working for free, Elion began to receive $20 per week for her work as a chemist. She saved her money and, with her parents' help, she enrolled in graduate school in 1939. She earned her master's degree in chemistry in 1941.

During World War II, there was a shortage of chemists, so jobs were open to women. Elion's first real lab job was conducting analytical quality control for the A&P food company. She learned a lot about instrumentation but eventually became restless. She was offered a position in a research lab—as an assistant to George Hitchings.

This was a wonderful opportunity because Elion was able to take on more and more responsibility as her career advanced. In 1967, she was named head of the Department of Experimental Therapy, a position she held until her retirement in 1983.

During her career, Elion worked on rational drug design, focusing especially on purine biochemistry and the development of drugs to help treat and cure diseases, including cancer. When she was awarded the Nobel Prize in 1988, she was happy but said that her real satisfaction had come from all of the people she had helped. More important to her than the Nobel Prize were the individuals whose lives she had saved or improved as seen in this letter from a grateful parent:

Dear Ms. Elion,

While reading the article about your Nobel Prize, I was overcome with a sense of trembling and amazement. I have a little boy who

(continues)

GERTRUDE B. ELION

(continued)

was diagnosed two years ago with acute lymphocytic leukemia. Since that time, he takes every night two pills of 6-mercaptopurine, better known to us in our family as 6-MP. My son and I long wondered who was responsible for this wonderful gift. We now know. And so it is with inexpressible gratitude for having contributed to the saving of one human life so very dear to me and so many other human lives that I write to say to you in the simplest, and hence the most profound and sincere of terms, thank you!

— Rabbi P.[9]

termed **epigenetic**. It does not entail a permanent change of the DNA. Epigenetic changes of genes do not alter the DNA sequence, but they can be passed on during cell division.

The fact that tumor suppressor gene and proto-oncogene functions can be rendered dysfunctional even when no mutation has occurred explains some interesting observations that have been made about *BRCA1* and *BRCA2*, the genes associated with hereditary breast and ovarian cancers. As described in Chapter 6, the inheritance of the mutant form of either or both of these genes increases an individual's cancer risk tremendously. Since these genes encode for proteins that are critical for DNA repair and tumor suppression, this increased likelihood of cancer comes as no surprise. What may seem unexpected, however, is that the breast tumor cells of people with sporadic breast cancers have *not* had mutant *BRCA1* or *BRCA2*. In fact, both genes had normal structures. In other cases of inherited cancers, such as retinoblastoma, a mutant version of the gene was also seen in the sporadic cancers. What was the explanation for *BRCA1* and *BRCA2* and breast cancer?

The answer to this question came from experiments that examined the *functions* of the *BRCA1* and *BRCA2* genes rather than just their structures. Scientists found that although normal versions of these genes were found in sporadic breast cancer cells, the genes appeared to be inactivated. Specifically, researchers compared *BRCA1* and *BRCA2* gene expression in breast cancer and normal cells and found that these genes were not functioning in the cancer cells. The scientists also demonstrated that the DNA had been chemically modified, but the modification was reversible. There was no permanent alteration of the genes themselves. It remains to be seen exactly how the activities of *BRCA1* and *BRCA2* were shut off in these cancer cells. These study results are important because they show that when physicians attempt to detect and diagnose cancer, they need to look beyond whether mutant genes are present and consider gene function as well.

Prevention

Although the future appears quite promising with respect to the development of improved methods for early detection and diagnosis of cancer, as well as its treatment, it is important to understand that prevention is the most powerful tool we have. No matter how good detection and treatment become, cancer will still cause physical and emotional suffering. Medical testing and care are also expensive, and equal access to them will always be difficult. The ideal situation is to avoid the development of cancer in the first place. Perhaps one of the best outcomes of the research on cancer genetics will be the identification of general cancer susceptibility genes that would help people learn more about how to reduce their individual risk of developing cancer. This information would add to the tremendous amount we already know about how to prevent cancer.

SUMMARY

Our understanding of the basic science of cancer—including the roles of oncogenes, tumor suppressors, and chromosomes—has produced new and improved methods for the detection, diagnosis, and treatment of cancer. It is likely that this knowledge will also improve our ability to prevent cancer in the future. Research will continue to focus on learning more about the genes involved in carcinogenesis and on the cell communication and regulatory pathways involved in the regulation of cell proliferation, differentiation, and survival. Work will also continue to focus on the development of even better methods for early detection, successful treatment, and most importantly, prevention.

ENDNOTES

◆

1. Shay, Jerry, and Woodring E. Wright, "Hayflick, His Limit, and Cellular Aging," *Nature Reviews Molecular Cell Biology* 1 (2000): 72–76.

2. Bishop, J. Michael. *How to Win the Nobel Prize*. Cambridge, Mass: Harvard University Press, 2003, p. 154.

3. "Elizabeth Blackburn Tells All About Telomeres," Sciencewatch.com. Available online. URL: http://www.sciencewatch.com/interviews/elizabeth_blackburn1.htm. Accessed October 19, 2006.

4. Greaves, Mel. *Cancer: The Evolutionary Legacy*. Oxford, England: Oxford University Press, 2001, p. 143.

5. Greaves, *Cancer*, p. 143.

6. Greaves, *Cancer*, p. 143.

7. Sidransky, David. "Advances in Cancer Detection," *Scientific American*. 275, no. 3 (1996): pp. 104–109.

8. The Nobel Foundation. "George H. Hitchings—Autobiography." Nobelprize.org. Available online. URL: http://nobelprize.org/nobel_prizes/medicine/laureates/1988/hitchings-autobio.html. Accessed October 19, 2006.

9. McGrayne, Sharon Bertsch. *Nobel Prize Women in Science*, 2nd ed. Secaucus, N.J.: Citadel Press Books, 1998, p. 282.

GLOSSARY

◆

adenoma   A benign tumor of epithelial tissue

adenocarcinoma   A malignant tumor of epithelial tissue

amino acid   Molecule that is the building block of protein

amplification   The process whereby genes replicate themselves multiple times and insert these copies into a cell's chromosome

angiogenic growth factors   Chemicals that promote the growth of new blood vessels

apoptosis   Programmed cell death

apoptotic proteins   Specific types of proteins that trigger cells to commit suicide

benign   Noncancerous

cancer   The breakdown of proper cell behavior and uncontrolled cell proliferation that results in the development of tumors that can spread throughout the body

carcinogen   A substance that causes cancer

carcinogenesis   The complex, multistep, gradual process by which cancer forms

carcinoma   Cancer of epithelial cells

cell culture   The growth of cells outside the body, in petri dishes, or flasks

chromosomes   The structures in cells that carry the genes

coding   Also called encoding; the process by which genetic information is transferred or assigned to a protein

contact-inhibition   The decrease in cell division or movement that occurs when cells touch one another

culture   To grow cells or tissue outside of the human body

cyst   A sac filled with fluid secretions and lodged beneath the skin surface

cytogenetics   The examination and analysis of the structure of chromosomes in cells

deletion   The loss of DNA from a chromosome

density-dependent inhibition   The phenomenon whereby cell proliferation stops when cell density reaches a specific level

differentiation   The specialization of cells into specific types of cells

DNA   Deoxyribonucleic acid; the molecule that carries genetic information

enzyme   A protein that facilitates or speeds up chemical reactions in the body

epigenetic   Referring to a change in cell behavior or function due to temporary changes in the function of genes

eugenics   The historically elitist study of the improvement of human genetics by selective breeding

familial   Refers to cancers where hereditary factors, but not a specific gene, may interact with environmental factors to produce cancer

familial adenomatous polyposis (FAP)   A type of colon cancer for which there is an inherited susceptibility

fibroblasts   Cells that produce connective or support tissues for the body

genes   Inherited instructions made up of DNA that influence or regulate the normal behavior of cells, including cell division

gerontology   The study of aging at the cellular level

growth factors   Small molecules, usually proteins, that act as chemical signals to trigger cell division

hereditary   Referring to cancers where there is a very strong family history of the disease and multiple members of either side of the family and from multiple generations develop the cancer

hypoxia   Inadequate oxygen availability

immortal   Refers to cancer cells having no finite lifespan

initiation   The first stage of tumor induction by a carcinogen

invasive   Refers to the spread of cancer cells from one part of the body to another

leukemia   A type of cancer or malignancy that involves the white blood cells

lymphoma   A type of cancer or malignancy involving enlargement of the lymph nodes, spleen, and liver

malignant   Cancers that grow uncontrollably and spread to other tissues in the body

mapping   Determining the physical location of genes on chromosomes

median   The middle of a range of numbers

melanoma   A highly aggressive, invasive skin cancer

metastasize   To spread cancer cells from a primary tumor to other places in the body

microarray   A technique in which the expression of many genes can be monitored simultaneously

mitotic spindle   Cellular structure that sorts and arranges chromosomes during cell division

monoclonal antibody A type of protein produced by the immune system that binds to only one kind of molecule, produced using a cell fusion procedure

mutation A change or error in DNA

mycoplasma A type of microorganism that causes pneumonia

nucleotide A type of molecule that is the building block of DNA

oncogene Cancer-causing gene

oncogenic Causing cancer

osteosarcoma Bone cancer

pathway A series of interconnected steps or events that facilitate cell function

pedigree A family tree that records the genetics of parents and off-spring over many generations

point mutation The alteration of one nucleotide in the DNA sequence of a gene

polio A viral disease that produces inflammation of the central nervous system

polyps Benign tumors

progression The development of increasing malignancy in a tumor

proliferation Abnormal cell division to produce new cells

promotion The stimulation of tumor formation in initiated cells

proteases Enzymes that digest protein

proteins Molecules in cells that are essential for cell structure and function

proto-oncogenes Normal cellular genes that encode molecules that regulate cell division, survival, or differentiation, and can be altered to become oncogenes

receptor A protein that binds to another molecule to initiate some sort of cellular response

reciprocal translocation A process by which two chromosomes exchange pieces with each other

retinoblastoma A childhood cancer of the retina, the light-gathering structure of the eye

Rous sarcoma virus (RSV) An example of a tumorigenic virus

rubella A contagious viral disease that produces a type of measles (sometimes called German measles) and can cause birth defects if a pregnant woman is infected

sarcoma A type of cancer of the bone, muscle, or connective tissue

secondary tumors Cancers that metastasize, or form at sites other than the original location of a tumor

signal molecule A molecule that operates either inside or outside cells to mediate cell communication

signal transducer A molecule that relays a signal from one molecule to the next in a cell communication pathway

somatic cell genetics The method of using cell fusion techniques to research chromosome function

sporadic Refers to cases of cancer where there is no family history of the disease

strain A group of cells that have identical or very similar characteristics

telomerase The enzyme that is responsible for replicating the telomeres, or the ends of chromosomes

telomeres Protective structures at the ends of chromosomes that are composed of a repeating sequence of nucleotides

tissue culture   The growth of groups of cells, or tissues, outside the body in petri dishes or flasks

transcription factors   Proteins that regulate gene activity

transform   To change a cell from a healthy to a cancerous one

translocation   The movement of a piece of chromosome to another chromosomal position

tumor   An abnormal mass of cells

tumorigenic   Prone to developing tumors

tumorigenesis   Development of a tumor

tumor suppressor   A substance that stops the growth and development of a tumor

ultraviolet (UV) light   A type of radiation that has higher energy than visible light but less than an X-ray

vaccines   Treatments in which weakened or dead disease-causing microorganisms are administered to prevent infection by a specific microorganism

virus   A parasite much smaller than a cell

xeroderma pigmentosum (XP)   Inherited type of skin cancer disorder caused by inability to repair DNA

FURTHER RESOURCES

◆

Bibliography

Academy of Achievement. "Interview: Bert Vogelstein, M.D., Cancer Researcher." Achievement.org. Available online. URL: http://www.achievement. org/autodoc/printmember/vog0int-1. Accessed on November 9, 2005.

——. "Profile: Bert Vogelstein, M.D., Cancer Researcher." Achievement. org. Available online. URL: http://www.achievement.org/autodoc/ printmember/vog0pro-1. Accessed on November 9, 2005.

Access Excellence. "Harold Elliot Varmus (1939–)." Accessexcellence.org. Available online. URL: http://www.accessexcellence.org/RC/AB/BC/ Harold_Elliot_Varmus.html. Downloaded December 14, 2005.

——. "J. Michael Bishop (1936–)." Accessexcellence.org. Available online. URL: http://www.accessexcellence.org/RC/AB/BC/J_Michael_ Bishop.html. Downloaded December 14, 2005.

Ageless Animals.com. "Biography: Leonard Hayflick." Agelessanimals.org. Available online. URL: http://www.agelessanimals.com/hayflickbio. htm. Downloaded February 14, 2005.

Alberts, Bruce, Dennis Bray, Julian Lewis, Martin Raff, Keith Roberts, and James D. Watson. *Molecular Biology of the Cell*, 3rd ed. New York: Garland Publishing, Inc., 1994.

Altshuler, M. L., S. E. Severin, and A. I. Glukhov. "The Tumor Cell Telomerase." *Biochemistry* [Moscow] 68, no. 12 (2003): 1275–1283.

American Society of Cell Biology. "ASCB Profile: J. Michael Bishop." ascb. org. Available online. URL: http://www.ascb.org/profiles/bishop.html. Downloaded December 14, 2005.

American Society of Pediatric Hematology/Oncology. "Distinguished Career Award 1999: Alfred G. Knudson, Jr., MD PhD." Aspho.org. Available online. URL: http://www.aspho.org/i4a/pages/index.cfm?pageid=206. Downloaded December 6, 2005.

Annenberg/CPB. "Elizabeth Blackburn, Ph.D." learner.org. Available online. URL: http://www.learner.org/channel/course/biology/units/cancer/experts. Accessed December 6, 2005.

Armstrong, Katrina. "Genetic Susceptibility to Breast Cancer: From the Roll of the Dice to the Hand Women Were Dealt." *Journal of the American Medical Association* 285, no. 22 (2005): 2907–2909.

BBC. "Moon Children." *Bbc.co.uk*. Available online. URL: http://www.bbc.co.uk/science/horizon/1999/moonchild-script.shtml. Downloaded February 14, 2005.

Becker, Wayne M., Lewis J. Kleinsmith, and Jeff Hardin. *The World of the Cell*, 6th ed. New York: Pearson-Benjamin Cummings, 2006.

Bennett, Ian C., Michael Gattas, and Bin Tean The. "The Genetic Basis of Breast Cancer and Its Clinical Implications." *ANZ Journal of Surgery* 69 (1999): 95–105.

Benowitz, Steven I. *Cancer*. Berkeley Heights, N.J.: Enslow Publishers, Inc., 1999.

Bishop, J. Michael. *How to Win the Nobel Prize*. Cambridge, Mass.: Harvard University Press, 2003.

Bocchetta, Maurizio, and Michele Carbone. "Epidemiology and Molecular Pathology at Crossroads to Establish Causation: Molecular Mechanisms of Malignant Transformation." *Oncogene* 23 (2004): 6484–6491.

Bozzone, D.M. *Causes of Cancer*. New York: Chelsea House Publishers, 2007.

Cairns, John. *Matters of Life and Death: Perspectives on Public Health, Molecular Biology, Cancer, and the Prospects for the Human Race*. Princeton, N.J.: Princeton University Press, 1997.

Cavenee, Webster K., and Raymond L. White. "The genetic basis of cancer." *Scientific American* 272, no. 3 (1995): 72–79.

Charames, George S., and Bharati Bapat. "Genomic Instability and Cancer." *Current Molecular Medicine* 3 (2003): 589–596.

CML Help.org. "The Faulty Gene Behind Chronic Myeloid Leukemia." *Cmlhelp.org*. Available online. URL: http://www.cmlhelp.org/webcast_transcrip.asp?b=cmlhelp&f=leukemia. Downloaded October 14, 2005.

———. "What Is Chronic Myeloid Leukemia?" *cmlhelp.org*. Available online. URL: http://www.cmlhelp.org/cml/intro.htm. Downloaded October 12, 2005.

Collins, Francis. "An Interview with Janet Rowley." *Laskerfoundation.org*. Available online. URL: http://www.laskerfoundation.org/arards/library/1998c_int_jr2.shtml. Downloaded December 6, 2005.

Cooper, Geoffrey M. *The Cell: A Molecular Approach*, 2nd Ed. Washington, D.C.: ASM Press, 2000.

Debernardi, Silvana, Debra Lillington, and Bryan Young. "Understanding Cancer at the Chromosome Level: 40 years of Progress." *European Journal of Cancer* 40 (2004): 1960–1967.

DiBacco, Alessandra, Karen Keeshan, Sharon L. McKenna, and Thomas G. Cotter. "Molecular Abnormalities in Chronic Myeloid Leukemia: Deregulation of Cell Growth and Apoptosis." *The Oncologist* 5 (2005): 405–415.

DNAdirect: Your Genes in Context. "Breast and Ovarian Cancer: How Are Breast and Ovarian Cancer Inherited?" *dnadirect.com*. Available online. URL: http://www.dnadirect.com/resource/conditions/breast_cancer/GH_Brca_. Downloaded July 8, 2005.

Dumitrescu, R. G., and I. Cotarla. "Understanding breast cancer risk–where do we stand in 2005?" *Journal of Cellular and Molecular Medicine Cell* 9, no. 1 (2005): 208–211.

Ellisen, Leif W., and Daniel A. Haber. "Hereditary Breast Cancer." *Annual Review of Medicine* 49 (1998): 425–436.

Ewald, Paul W. *Plague Time: The New Germ Theory of Disease*. New York: Anchor Books, 2002.

Eye Cancer Network. "Retinoblastoma." *Eyecancer.com*. Available online. URL: http://www.eyecancer.com/conditions/Retinal%20Tumors/retino. html. Downloaded July 7, 2005.

———. "Retinoblastoma Genetics." *Eyecancer.com*. Available online. URL: http://www.eyecancer.com/conditions/Retinal%20Tumors/retinog. html. Downloaded July 7, 2005.

———. "Retinoblastoma and Secondary Cancers." *Eyecancer.com*. Available online. URL: http://www.eyecancer.com/conditions/Retinal%20Tumors/ retinos.html. Downloaded July 7, 2005.

Fearnhead, Nicola S., Michael P. Britton, and Walter Bodmer. "The ABC of APC." *Human Molecular Genetics* 10, no. 7 (2001): 721–733.

Feinberg, Andrew P. "The Epigenetics of Cancer Etiology." *Seminars in Cancer Biology* 12 (2004): 427–432.

Feldser, David M., Jennifer A., and Carol Greider. "Telomere Dysfunction and the Initiation of Genomic Instability." *Nature Reviews Cancer* 3 (2003): 1–5.

Fodde, Riccardo, Ron Smits, and Hans Clevers. "*APC*, Signal Transduction and Genetic Instability in Colorectal Cancer." *Nature Reviews Cancer* 1 (2001): 55–67.

Friedberg, Errol C. "How Nucleotide Excision Repair Protects Against Cancer." *Nature Reviews Cancer* 1 (2001): 22–33.

Gibbs, W. Wayt. "Untangling the Roots of Cancer." *Scientific American* 289, no. 1 (2003): 56–65.

Goodsell, David S. "The Molecular Perspective: The *ras* Oncogene." *The Oncologist* 4 (1999): 263–264.

———. "The Molecular Perspective: The *src* Oncogene." *The Oncologist* 6 (2001): 474–476.

Greaves, Mel. *Cancer: The Evolutionary Legacy*. New York: Oxford University Press, Inc., 2001.

Greider, Carol W., and Elizabeth Blackburn. "Telomeres, Telomerase and Cancer." *Scientific American* 274, no. 2 (1996): 92–97.

Hahn, William C., and Robert A. Weinberg. "Rules for Making Human Tumor Cells." *New England Journal of Medicine* 347, no. 20 (2002): 1593–1603.

Hall, Peter A. "*p53*: The Challenge of Linking Basic Science and Patient Management." *The Oncologist* 3 (1998): 218–224.

Harris, Henry. "Putting on the Brakes." *Nature* 427 (2004): 201.

Hemminki, Kari. "Genetic Epidemiology: Science and Ethics on Familial Cancers." *Acta Oncologica* 40, no. 4 (2001): 439–444.

Holtz, Andrew. "The Role of Genetic Mutations in Breast and Ovarian Cancers." *Nasw.org*. Available online. URL: http://nasw.org/users/holtza/SHNBRCA12.html. Downloaded November 11, 2005.

Klausne, Richard. "An Interview with Alfred Knudson." Laskerfoundation.org. Available online. URL: http://www.laskerfoundation.org/awards/library/199c_int_ak2.shtml. Downloaded December 6, 2005.

Knudson, Alfred G. "Chasing the Cancer Demon." *Annual Review of Genetics* 34 (2000): 1–9.

Kurzrock, Razelle, Hagop M. Kantarjian, Brian J. Druker, and Moshe Talpaz. "Philadelphia Chromosome—Positive Leukemias: From Basic Mechanisms to Molecular Therapeutics." *Annals of Internal Medicine* 138 (2003): 819–830.

Lasker Foundation. "Janet Rowley." *Laskerfoundation.org*. Available online. URL: http://www.laskerfoundation.org/awards/library/1998c_paper_jr.shtml. Downloaded December 6, 2005.

Latonen, Leena, and Marikki Laiho. "Cellular UV Damage Responses—Function of Tumor Suppressor *p53*." *Biochimica et Biophysica Acta* 1755 (2005): 71–89.

Leaf, Clifton. "Why We're Losing the War on Cancer (And How to Win It)." *Fortune* 149, no. 6 (2004): 76–97.

Lengauer Christoph, Kenneth W. Kinzler, and Bert Vogelstein. "Genetic Instabilities in Human Cancers." *Nature* 396 (1998): 643–649.